# Norway Travel Guide

The Complete Exploration Handbook to Plan Your Perfect Adventure to the Land of Endless Sunsets | Maximize Your Time with Local Insights & Detailed Itineraries

**Henning Gardner**

# Table of Contents

# ⭐ YOUR FREE GIFT ⭐

Discover the secrets of Norway with "Explore Norway: Specialized Journeys and Unique Discoveries," your essential guide to venturing into breathtaking landscapes and unique cultural experiences that only Norway can offer. Now available for free, this book is your key to immersing yourself in a world of tailor-made travel and surprising discoveries, easy to organize and incredibly enriching for your adventurous spirit. By simply scanning the QR Code below, you'll gain access to an exceptional collection of itineraries that will not only delight your sense of exploration but also guide you in discovering hidden treasures. Don't miss this opportunity to transform your journey into an unforgettable experience. Scan the QR Code now and start your journey towards discovering the most authentic and vibrant Norway!

**SCAN THE QR CODE TO DOWNLOAD THE EXPLORE NORWAY SPECIALIZED JOURNEYS AND UNIQUE DISCOVERIES' EBOOK**

# Introduction

Welcome to Norway, the land of natural wonders, where unforgettable experiences and breathtaking landscapes await you. Whether you're an outdoor enthusiast, a nature lover, or simply seeking a unique adventure, Norway has compelling reasons to be your travel destination of choice. Here's some basic information on Norway's geography, climate, culture, and practical tips to help you plan your trip.

**Geography:** Norway is a nation renowned for its breathtaking natural beauty. Its varied landscapes feature spectacular fjords, mighty mountains, lush forests, and gorgeous coastlines. The nation borders Sweden, Finland, and Russia and is situated in Northern Europe. There are numerous options for sailing and coastal exploration over the thousands of kilometers of coastline.

**Climate:** If you're planning to visit Norway in July, you're in for a treat as this month is the peak of summer in the country. July offers the best weather for outdoor activities, with warm and comfortable temperatures averaging around 20°C or more. The days are long, and in the northern part of Norway, you can experience the phenomenon of the midnight sun, where the sun never sets and provides incredible sunsets with red hues.

**Culture:** Norwegians are known for their strong connection to nature and outdoor activities. In July, many Norwegians take their summer holiday, leading to popular tourist spots being more crowded. This time offers a unique chance to experience local culture and participate in various festivals and events, such as St Olaf's Day celebrations and summer music festivals like Moldejazz and Trænafestivalen.

## Things to Do in Norway in July:

1. **Hiking:** July is an excellent time for hiking as the weather is favorable, and the hiking trails are open and operational. Popular hikes include Preikestolen, Trolltunga, and Jotunheimen. Don't forget to bring sunscreen and a jacket for windy conditions.

2. **Swimming and Beaches:** Take advantage of the warm July weather to enjoy swimming in the freshwater lakes, fjords, and ocean beaches. Norway's beaches attract locals and tourists alike, providing a relaxing break from all the hiking.

3. **Experience the Midnight Sun:** Head to Northern Norway to witness the mesmerizing midnight sun, where the sun stays above the horizon for most of the day. Locations like Bodø and further north offer this unique experience.

4. **Explore the Fjords:** Cruise or kayak through dramatic fjords like Nærøyfjord, a UNESCO-listed site, and admire majestic waterfalls like the Seven Sisters and Bridal Veil.

5. **Visit Charming Villages and Cities:** Explore Oslo, the capital city, and its highlights and museums. Head west to see the glittering fjords, visit charming villages like Flåm, and explore historic cities like Bergen and Trondheim.

## Practical Tips:

- Book Accommodation in Advance: Since July is a popular travel month, it is best to reserve your lodging far in advance to guarantee availability.
- Pack for Variable Weather: While July offers warm days, be prepared for some rainy days and possibly windy conditions, especially in the mountains.
- Transportation: Norway has an extensive network of trains, buses, and regional airlines that make it easy to explore the country. Consider using Norway in a Nutshell® tour or Hurtigruten Coastal Voyage for an unforgettable journey.
- Local Cuisine: Don't miss out on trying traditional Norwegian dishes like salmon, reindeer, and rømmegrøt (a sour cream porridge).

Remember that Norway offers a myriad of adventures and experiences that will make your journey unforgettable. So, whether you're hiking along scenic trails, basking on sandy beaches, or marveling at the midnight sun, Norway promises a once-in-a-lifetime experience. Enjoy your travel to Norway and create cherished memories amid its natural wonders!

# How To Can You Help This book?

Composing this book has proven to be quite a challenge in fact, debugging for hours feels easier than the process of writing. For the first time in my life, I've encountered writer's block. Understanding the topics is one thing, but attempting to articulate them in a logical, concise, cohesive, and well-organized manner is an entirely different task.

Furthermore, since I've chosen to steer clear of any publishing houses, I can proudly label myself as an "independent author." This is a personal decision that hasn't been without its difficulties, but my dedication to helping others has prevailed.

That's why I would be immensely grateful if you could provide feedback on Amazon. Your input would mean a great deal to me and would go a long way in sharing this material with others. I recommend the following:

1. **If you haven't already, scan the QR code** at the start of the book and download THE SPECIALIZED TRIPS AND UNIQUE EXPERIENCES IN NORWAY IN OUR EBOOK
2. **Scan the QR code below and quickly leave feedback on Amazon!**

# SCAN ME

The optimal approach? Share a short video where you discuss your thoughts on the book! If that feels like too much, there's absolutely no pressure. Providing feedback along with a couple of photos of the book would still be greatly appreciated!

**Note:** There's no obligation whatsoever, but it would be immensely valued!

I'm thrilled to embark on this journey with you. Are you prepared to delve in?

Enjoy your reading!

# Chapter 1:

# Trip Preparation

Planning a trip to Norway can be a truly enchanting experience, given the country's breathtaking beauty and abundant natural wonders.

The following travel necessities should be considered while packing for a trip to Norway:

**Most Suitable Time To Go.**

Depending on your interests and the experiences you want to enjoy, there is no one optimum time to travel to Norway. Here is a detailed reference on the best seasons to travel to Norway and the varying opening times for the country's greatest sights:

**1. High Season (Mid-June to Mid-August):** This period is ideal for outdoor activities, hiking, and exploring Norway's stunning landscapes. The weather is generally warm and sunny, making it perfect for outdoor adventures. However, popular destinations can be crowded, and it's essential to plan your itinerary and accommodations in advance.

**2. Shoulder Season (May - Mid-June, Mid-August to September):** The fall is a fantastic time to explore Norway's fjords because there are less tourists and the weather is still pleasant. However, rates for lodging can be expensive, particularly on weekends and during festival seasons. To enjoy beautiful weather and less traffic, think about going during the shoulder season.

**3. Low Season (October to April):** This period is perfect for experiencing the magical Northern Lights. While it can be bitterly cold during this time, you have a higher chance of witnessing the aurora borealis. Many attractions may be closed, and daylight hours are shorter, but seasonal accommodation deals are available, making it a more budget-friendly option.

**4. Spring (March to May):** Spring is still chilly, but the weather is gradually warming up, and the days are getting longer. This season is great for snow activities like skiing, and it's an excellent time to visit before the summer tourist crowds arrive.

**5. Summer (June to August):** This is the peak tourist season in Norway, with long days and pleasant weather. It's the perfect time for hiking, exploring the fjords, and enjoying outdoor activities. However, popular attractions may be crowded, and accommodation and flights might cost more during this time.

**6. Fall (September to November):** Fall offers milder weather, and it's an excellent time to save money on lodging and flights compared to peak season. The Northern Lights season begins in October, and you can still enjoy sightseeing and outdoor activities before the winter sets in.

**7. Winter (December to February):** Winter in Norway means short days with limited daylight, but it's an opportunity to witness the mesmerizing Northern Lights. Skiing and snowboarding enthusiasts will enjoy the slopes, and indoor activities like museum visits are also popular during this time

## Timelines for Top Attractions

- **Northern Lights:** The best time to see the Northern Lights is generally from September to October and February to March. These months offer darker skies, providing an increased chance of witnessing the aurora borealis. The snowy landscapes during this time add to the magical experience.
- **Fjords:** Norway's fjords are primarily a seasonal destination, and many attractions, hotels, campsites, and roads are closed during the winter months. However, visiting the fjords in winter can be a special experience if you plan and are flexible.
- **Hiking and Outdoor Activities:** The high season (mid-June to

mid-August) is the best time for hiking and outdoor adventures. The pleasant weather and long daylight hours make it ideal for exploring Norway's natural wonders.

- **Winter Sports:** Skiing and snowboarding enthusiasts can enjoy the snowy season from January to March. Ski resorts open as soon as the first snow falls, and February and March are popular months for winter sports due to the lighter days.

- **Midnight Sun:** If you want to experience the Midnight Sun, visit Norway during the summer months, especially in June and July. In the northern regions, you can witness sunshine around the clock, providing ample time for outdoor activities.

By considering the different timelines for top attractions and the best time for your preferred activities, you can plan a memorable trip to Norway that aligns with your interests and desires. Keep in mind that the weather can vary across regions, so pack accordingly and be prepared for possible changes in climate during your visit.

## Itineraries

Below are three different Norway itineraries, each offering a unique way to explore this stunning destination.

### Norway Itinerary: 7 Days of Breathtaking Beauty (May Cause Wanderlust)

- Day 1: Arrive in Oslo and explore the vibrant city with its beautiful landscapes, museums, and historical sites. Enjoy local cuisine and settle into your accommodation in Oslo.

- Day 2-4: Travel from Oslo to Flam, where you can experience the scenic rail journey through the picturesque countryside. Spend three nights in Flam, exploring the stunning fjords and enjoying outdoor activities like hiking and kayaking.

- Day 5: Travel from Flam to Bergen, a charming city with colorful houses and a rich cultural heritage. Explore the city's attractions and enjoy the local cuisine.

- Day 6-7: Return to Oslo via Bergen, where you can spend the last two days exploring more of the city's highlights, relaxing in parks, or visiting museums before departing.

## 9-Day Norway Itinerary (Earth Curious)

- Day 1-2: Begin your journey in Bergen, a city known for its artistic charm and surrounded by breathtaking landscapes. Explore the city's historic wharf and museums.

- Day 3-4: Travel to Balestrand, a serene destination located on the Sognefjord. Enjoy the peaceful ambiance, take in stunning views, and explore nearby attractions.

- Day 5-6: Continue to Flåm, a place known for its scenic railway and picturesque surroundings. Engage in outdoor activities and immerse yourself in the natural beauty of the area.

- Day 7: Travel from Flåm to Oslo and explore the vibrant capital city's cultural offerings and architectural wonders.

- Day 8-9: Conclude your trip in Oslo, delving deeper into the city's

13

highlights, museums, and parks before heading back home.

**12-Day Norway Road Trip Itinerary (Traveling Canucks)**

- Day 1: Start your road trip in Oslo, and explore the city's fascinating architecture and attractions.
- Day 2-3: Drive to Hemsedal, a beautiful mountain village, and enjoy outdoor activities such as hiking and skiing.
- Day 4: Visit Borgund and its iconic stave church before continuing to Aurland to witness the stunning Aurlandsfjord.
- Day 5-6: Explore the picturesque village of Flam and the majestic Geirangerfjord, known for its breathtaking views.
- Day 7-8: Head to Bergen and discover the city's colorful houses and cultural delights.
- Day 9: Travel to Forde and enjoy the tranquil surroundings and landscapes.
- Day 10-11: Visit Jostedalsbreen National Park, home to impressive glaciers and scenic beauty.
- Day 12: Return to Oslo and conclude your road trip with more exploration in the capital city.

Each of these itineraries offers a fantastic opportunity to experience Norway's natural beauty, vibrant cities, and unique culture. Consider your interests, preferred mode of travel, and available time to choose the itinerary that suits you best. Whether you're exploring fjords, hiking mountains, or immersing yourself in city life, a trip to Norway promises to be an unforgettable adventure.

14

# What to Pack

When packing for a trip to Norway, it's important to consider the weather, activities, and the season you'll be visiting. Here's a comprehensive packing list that combines the essential items from the provided sources:

1. Clothing:

- Layered clothing: Norway's weather can be unpredictable, so pack lightweight layers that you can easily add or remove.
- Waterproof and windproof jacket: Norway is known for its rain, so a waterproof jacket will keep you dry during outdoor activities.
- Warm sweaters and long-sleeved shirts: Even in summer, temperatures can be cool, especially in the evenings.
- Comfortable pants and jeans: Choose durable and versatile pants for outdoor activities and casual outings.
- Waterproof and sturdy hiking boots: Norway's terrain calls for good-quality hiking boots for comfortable exploration.
- Warm socks: Pack wool or thermal socks for added warmth and comfort during hikes.
- Hat, gloves, and scarf: These are essential for colder seasons when visiting higher altitudes or engaging in winter activities.
- Swimwear: If you plan to visit the fjords or go swimming in lakes or coastal areas during the summer.

2. Accessories and Gear:

- Daypack: A lightweight and water-resistant daypack will come in handy for hikes and day trips.
- Lifestraw Water Bottle: Stay hydrated with a reusable water bottle with a built-in filter, especially for remote areas.
- Packing Cubes: Keep your clothing organized and easily accessible with packing cubes.
- Power adapter: Norway uses Type C or Type F plugs, so bring a universal power adapter to charge your electronic devices.
- Virtual Private Network (VPN): Ensure secure internet access while traveling by using a VPN.
- Windproof Travel Umbrella: Pack a compact travel umbrella for unexpected rain showers.
- Lipstick-sized Portable Charger: Keep your devices charged on the go with a portable charger.
- Hiking Gear: If you plan on hiking, bring a sturdy backpack, hiking boots, and appropriate clothing for outdoor activities.

3. Miscellaneous:

- Travel documents: Passport, ID, travel insurance, and copies of important documents.
- Medications and first aid kit: Carry any necessary medications and a basic first aid kit.
- Toiletries: Bring your personal toiletries, including sunscreen, insect repellent, and any specific items you require.
- Travel towel: Pack a lightweight and quick-drying towel for outdoor activities.

- Snacks: Have some energy bars or snacks for long hikes or when food options are limited.
- Cash and cards: Bring a mix of cash and cards for convenience.

Remember to check the specific season and weather conditions for your travel dates and adjust your packing accordingly. It's always a good idea to pack light and be prepared for various weather scenarios.

## Entry Requirements

The following are the prerequisites for entering Norway:

1. COVID-19 Restrictions: As of February 12, 2022, Norway no longer has any travel restrictions. Upon arriving in Norway, there are no formalities for screening, quarantine, or registration. Additionally, the requirement to finish entry registration and present a clean COVID-19 test result before arrival has been lifted.

2. Entry criteria for Norway are the same for all visitors, regardless of whether they have received their COVID-19 immunization. Entry to Norway does not require proof of immunization status. The same is true if COVID-19 was administered during the last 12 months; there are no unique requirements depending on COVID-19 history.

3. Validity of Passport: If you are a British citizen coming to Norway, your passport must have been issued no more than ten years prior to the date you enter the country and must remain valid for at least three months after the day you want to depart. Similar

restrictions on passport validity apply if you intend to travel to Norway from within the Schengen region.

4. Visa Requirements: Americans do not need a visa to enter Norway for quick trips like business meetings or vacations that last up to 90 days in any 180-day period. You must meet Norway's entry requirements and may need a visa and/or work permit if you plan to remain longer, work, study, or for other particular reasons. If you're visiting without a visa, be sure the entire trip fits within the 90-day window.

5. Transiting through Norway: Before leaving, confirm with your airline if you will be passing through Norway en route to your final destination.

6. Pets: It is advisable to check with the Norwegian Embassy in London for special rules and procedures if you intend to bring pets with you.

It is always essential to stay updated on any changes to entry requirements, especially related to COVID-19 regulations, before traveling. Travelers should also consider checking with the Norwegian embassy, high commission, or consulate for the most current and accurate information regarding entry rules and requirements.

## Travel Tips

### 1. Safety

Norway is usually regarded as a safe destination. To guarantee your safety, you should always be conscious of your surroundings and take the appropriate precautions. Here are some safety advice and details for travelers to Norway:

- Low Crime Rate: Violent crime is not common in Norway, which has a low crime rate. Petty thefts and burglary of homes and businesses are the most likely types of crime. In popular tourist sites, hotel lobbies, train and transit terminals, and nearby places, pickpocketing and small-time theft can happen more regularly. It's best to be on guard and watch your possessions, especially in crowded areas. Pickpockets and bag snatchers are known to frequent the Oslo Central train station.

- As with any European nation, Norway has a low overall risk of terrorism, but transnational terrorist organizations could pose a concern. The governments of Europe take measures to prevent terrorist attacks, but foreigners are warned to exercise caution when it comes to their personal protection.

- Fraudsters: Just like in other well-known tourist location, you should use caution while dealing with scams. Learn about common travel frauds and be wary of anyone seeking to take advantage of you. For information on scams, it is suggested to visit the Department of State and FBI pages.

- Emergency Services: Dial 112 to reach the local police in case of an emergency. Call 116 117 to reach the Norwegian medical service, which is available around-the-clock. Report any crimes you've been the victim of to the authorities in your area, and then

19

get help from the nearest American embassy.

- Domestic Violence: The U.S. Embassy can provide aid if you are a citizen of the United States and are experiencing domestic violence while abroad in Norway. Additionally, helplines with a variety of domestic abuse support services are accessible.
- Outdoor Security Natural scenery in Norway is a big draw, but it's necessary to be ready and practice outdoor safety. If you intend to participate in outdoor activities, be sure to learn about the risks involved in your preferred activity. Be prepared, follow safety precautions, and pay attention to the weather.

## 2. Health

The following essential points are included in the health advice for visitors to Norway:

1. Norway is completely open for travel as of the specified date, with no COVID-19 testing requirements or quarantines. While visiting the nation, visitors do not need to be concerned with face masks or other COVID-19-related issues.

2. Medical Aid: Calling the 24-hour Norwegian medical service at 116 117 will allow visitors to Norway to get advice and assistance if they feel any symptoms such a fever, sore throat, chest pain, or trouble breathing.

3. Even though Norway is an industrialized nation, diseases can still be transferred through insect bites. When spending time outside or in wooded regions, travelers are recommended to take care to

avoid being bitten by insects. Wearing long sleeves, long pants, and helmets, applying insect repellents with DEET or other suggested active ingredients, and examining the body for ticks after outdoor activities are some of these practices.

4. Safety Outdoors: Visitors who partake in outdoor activities in Norway should keep an eye on the weather as it changes and modify plans as necessary. It is crucial to include a basic first aid kit, dress appropriately, and pack safety gear like sunscreen and bug spray. Additionally important factors for safety during outdoor activities include hydration and UV protection.

5. Travelers should only swim in approved locations, heed warnings from lifeguards and flags posted on beaches, and avoid ingesting untreated water to avoid contracting waterborne diseases.

6. Animal Interaction: Although most animals in Norway stay away from people, it's still important to avoid wild animals since they may attack if they feel threatened, if they need to defend their young or territory, or if they are hurt or ill.

## 3. Currency and banking

- Currency: The Norwegian Krone is the country's official currency (NOK). Having some Norwegian Krone on hand is helpful for small purchases and locations that might not take credit cards. Airports, banks, and exchange offices all around the nation offer currency exchange services. It is advised to tip in local money and do modest transactions.

- Payment Methods: Due to its high level of digitization, Norway uses currency less frequently. Most establishments accept credit and debit cards, even those from other countries. To make sure your cards function properly while you're there, it's a good idea to let your bank or credit card provider know about your trip plans. Mobile payment apps and contactless payments are both frequently used.

- Currency Exchange: If you need to exchange currency, it's recommended to do so at banks or authorized exchange offices for better rates and lower fees. Wise (formerly TransferWise) offers a travel money card that allows you to load and spend Norwegian Krone at the real exchange rate, saving you money on currency conversion fee.

## 4. Language and communication

When visiting Norway, it's helpful to understand the local language and communication etiquette. Here are some points to consider:

1. Language: The official language of Norway is Norwegian. Most Norwegians are fluent in English, especially in urban areas and popular tourist destinations. English is widely spoken and understood, so you'll generally have no trouble communicating in English during your visit.
2. Basic Phrases: While English is commonly spoken, learning a few basic Norwegian phrases can be appreciated by locals and add to your cultural experience. Here are some useful phrases:
   - Hello: Hei (hay)

- Thank you: Takk (tahk)
- Please: Vær så snill (vair so snill)
- Excuse me: Unnskyld (oon-skuld)
- Yes: Ja (yah)
- No: Nei (nay)
- Goodbye: Ha det (hah deh)

3. Communication Etiquette: Norwegians value politeness and respect in their interactions. Here are some etiquette tips to keep in mind:

   - Greetings: When meeting someone, a handshake is the standard form of greeting. Maintain eye contact and address people using their titles and surnames unless you are invited to use their first names.

   - Personal Space: Norwegians appreciate personal space and tend to stand at an arm's length from each other during conversations. It's best to respect this cultural norm.

   - Punctuality: Norwegians value punctuality, so it's important to be on time for appointments and meetings. If you're running late, it's courteous to inform the person you're meeting.

# Chapter 2:

# Top Attractions

This Nordic nation is known for its outstanding natural beauty and boasts a wealth of interesting locations. Fjords, waterfalls, hiking routes, little towns tucked away beneath enormous mountains, and bustling cities may all be found in this region.

We've put up this list of Norway's best attractions to help you focus your bucket list.

**Exploring Oslo**

Oslo, the capital city of Norway, offers a range of tourism highlights, activities, and hidden gems. Here's a description of Oslo's attractions:

- Explore the well-preserved Viking ships and other items from the Viking Age at the Viking Ship Museum to learn more about the interesting history of Norway.

- Gustav Vigeland's approximately 200 sculptures can be found in the Vigeland Sculpture Park, which serves as a testament to his prodigious talent and inventiveness.

- The changing of the guard ritual is performed every day during the summer at the Royal Palace, which is the Norwegian monarch's official residence.

- Oslo Opera House is a magnificent piece of waterfront architecture. You can take in a concert or just savor the building's distinctive style.

- Discover the medieval castle and stronghold known as Akershus, which has protected Oslo for centuries. Views of the entire city can be had by ascending the tower.

- Explore the history of skiing at the Holmenkollen Ski Museum and Tower, then ascend for breath-taking views over Oslo and the surrounding area.

- Learn about the renowned polar exploration ship Fram and its journeys to the Arctic and Antarctic areas at the Fram Museum.

- The Nobel Peace Center: Learn about the lives of Nobel Peace Prize winners and see exhibitions that advance human rights and world peace.

- The Kon-Tiki Museum, the Fram Museum, and the Viking Ship Museum are all located on the Bygdy Peninsula.

- A magnificent collection of modern and contemporary works by

Norwegian and foreign artists may be found at the Astrup Fearnley Museum, a museum of contemporary art.

- Oslo Cathedral is a gorgeous cathedral in the center of Oslo with exquisite architecture and ornamentation.
- Aker Brygge is a waterfront neighborhood featuring a variety of stores, eateries, and pubs. It's a wonderful area to unwind, eat, and take in the scenery.
- The Munch Museum has well-known works including "The Scream" and is devoted to the paintings of renowned Norwegian artist Edvard Munch.
- Botanical Garden: A serene haven in the middle of the city, ideal for a leisurely stroll among a variety of plant species and picturesque vistas.
- Oslo City Hall: Take a tour of the building with a guide to see the striking murals and architecture. Each year, the Nobel Peace Prize ceremony takes place here.
- Grünerlkka is a thriving, fashionable district renowned for its cool cafes, shops, and street art.
- Ekebergparken Sculpture Park: Stroll through this open-air park to take in panoramic views of Oslo and take in the modern art pieces.
- The food hall Mathallen Oslo offers a variety of delectable treats, including fresh vegetables, handmade goods, and dishes from around the world.
- Oslo Fjord: To appreciate the scenic surroundings of the city, take a boat excursion or go for a leisurely walk along the fjord.

- Hiking in Nordmarka: Get away from the city and discover the forests of Nordmarka, which are close by and provide a variety of hiking paths, lakes, and beautiful scenery.

**The Fjords**

Norway is known for its spectacular fjords, each offering unique tourist highlights and experiences. Here are some of the notable fjords in Norway and their tourist highlights:

- Geirangerfjord: Geirangerfjord is one of the most famous fjords in Norway and a UNESCO World Heritage site. It features towering cliffs, cascading waterfalls like the Seven Sisters and the Bridal Veil, and breathtaking landscapes. Visitors can enjoy fjord sightseeing tours, kayaking, and hiking trails that offer panoramic views of the fjord and surrounding mountains.
- Nærøyfjord: Nærøyfjord is another UNESCO World Heritage site and is known for its dramatic and narrow landscape. It is surrounded by steep mountains and offers mesmerizing views. Visitors can take scenic boat cruises or kayak along the fjord to immerse themselves in its natural beauty.
- Aurlandsfjord: Aurlandsfjord is an arm of the Sognefjord and is often considered one of the most picturesque fjords in Norway. It is characterized by deep blue waters, lush green valleys, and charming villages like Flåm. Visitors can enjoy boat cruises, hiking trails, and the famous Flåm Railway, which offers stunning views of the fjord and surrounding landscapes.

- Lysefjord: Lysefjord is located in southwestern Norway and is known for its dramatic cliffs, including the famous Preikestolen (Pulpit Rock) and Kjerag. These landmarks attract hikers and adventure seekers from around the world. Visitors can take boat tours to explore the fjord and witness its towering rock formations.

- Hardangerfjord: Hardangerfjord is the third-largest fjord in the world and offers a diverse range of attractions. It is famous for its fruit orchards, especially during the blooming season in spring. Visitors can explore charming villages like Lofthus, hike to breathtaking viewpoints, visit waterfalls like Vøringsfossen, and enjoy activities such as fjord cruises and kayaking.

- Trollfjord: Trollfjord is a narrow and scenic fjord located in the Lofoten Islands in northern Norway. It is known for its dramatic landscapes, steep mountains, and the possibility of encountering wildlife such as sea eagles and seals. Visitors can take boat tours to experience the beauty of Trollfjord and its surrounding mountains.

- Oslofjord: Oslofjord is a fjord that encircles Oslo, the nation of Norway's capital. It may not conform to the conventional definition of a fjord, but it nonetheless provides a distinctive coastal experience. Boat cruises, island hopping, swimming, and viewing sights like the Oscarsborg Fortress and quaint coastal towns like Drbak are all available to visitors.

**The Northern Lights**

The Northern Lights, also known as the Aurora Borealis, is a celestial wonder that captivates travelers from around the world. Norway is one of the best places to witness this breathtaking natural phenomenon, and the further north you go, the higher your chances of encountering this mesmerizing light display. Locations like Tromso, the North Cape, and the Lofoten Islands are renowned for providing awe-inspiring views of the Northern Lights during the months of October to March, when the nights are darker and the skies are clearer. It's during this time that travelers flock to Norway in search of this ethereal spectacle.

**The Best Time to Witness the Northern Lights**

To witness the Northern Lights at their most vibrant, visiting Norway between October and March is ideal. The dark winter nights during this period provide an optimal backdrop for the lights to illuminate the skies in their full glory. It's worth noting that the summer months bring the midnight sun to the north of Norway, which means it never gets completely dark, making it impossible to see the Northern Lights during this time.

**Factors Affecting Northern Lights Visibility**

Several factors play a significant role in the visibility of the Northern Lights:

1. **KP Index:** The KP index indicates the likelihood of seeing the Northern Lights in a particular area. The lower the latitude, the

higher the KP index needed to witness the lights. In northern Norway, even a KP strength of 1 can provide a good chance of seeing the lights.

2. **Weather Conditions:** Cloud coverage is a critical factor in observing the Northern Lights. Clear skies offer the best viewing opportunities, while heavy cloud cover may obstruct the view. Travelers are advised to check weather forecasts and head away from city lights to reduce light pollution.

3. **Darkness:** The longer the hours of darkness, the better the chances of seeing the Northern Lights. From October to March, Norway experiences shorter daylight hours, allowing for early sightings of the lights.

4. **Eyes Adaptation to Darkness:** Allowing your eyes to adjust to the dark enhances your ability to see the Northern Lights more clearly. Avoid looking at bright lights like phone screens while waiting for the lights to appear.

5. **Aurora Alert Apps:** Travelers can download Aurora alert apps to track the probability of the Northern Lights appearing. While not entirely accurate, these apps can help determine if waiting outside for the lights is worth the effort.

**Top Destinations to Witness the Northern Lights in Norway**

1. **The North Cape:** As the most northern point in all of Europe, the North Cape offers a unique vantage point to witness the Northern Lights. This extraordinary location provides an unforgettable experience amidst stunning natural beauty.

2. **Tromsø:** Known as the "Gateway to the Arctic," Tromsø is a vibrant city and a popular base for Northern Lights expeditions. Its location inside the Arctic Circle makes it an excellent starting point for chasing the lights in the Arctic countryside.

3. **Lofoten Islands:** This archipelago is not only a picturesque destination but also an excellent spot for Northern Lights enthusiasts. The combination of rugged landscapes and the dancing lights creates an otherworldly atmosphere.

4. **Narvik, Kirkenes, Alta, and Bodø:** These cities also offer great opportunities to see the Northern Lights. The experience is amazing, whether you're camping out in the Arctic wilderness or cuddling up in a traditional Sami tent.

**Northern Lights Activities**

Beyond simply witnessing the Northern Lights, travelers can engage in a variety of activities to enhance their experience:

- **Dog Sledding:** Experience the thrill of gliding through snowy landscapes pulled by a team of huskies, creating an authentic Arctic adventure.

- **Snowmobiling:** Explore the frozen wilderness on a snowmobile, venturing into the heart of Norway's icy landscapes.

- **Ice Fishing:** Engage in this traditional activity, dropping a line into icy waters in the hope of catching a prized Arctic fish.

- **Whale Watching:** Witness majestic marine creatures, such as killer whales and humpback whales, as they migrate through Norwegian waters.
- **Cross-Country Skiing:** Glide through pristine winter trails, surrounded by breathtaking snow-covered landscapes.
- **Photography Courses:** Learn how to capture the elusive beauty of the Northern Lights with expert photography courses.
- **Visiting an Ice Hotel:** Experience the magical atmosphere of an ice hotel, spending the night in a frosty wonderland.

**Hidden Gems for Northern Lights Enthusiasts**

While the popular destinations offer unforgettable experiences, some hidden gems in Norway provide unique and less-crowded encounters with the Northern Lights:

- **Senja:** Known as Norway's second-largest island, Senja boasts dramatic landscapes and clear skies, making it a lesser-known Northern Lights paradise.
- **Svalbard (Spitsbergen):** Although farther from the typical Northern Lights belt, Svalbard offers the chance to witness the lights in mid-winter, complemented by stunning Arctic wilderness.
- **Lyngen Alps:** This picturesque mountain range presents an excellent backdrop for the Aurora Borealis, combined with opportunities for snow sports and mountain adventures.
- **Hamnøy:** A tiny fishing village in the Lofoten Islands, Hamnøy

provides an idyllic setting for viewing the Northern Lights, surrounded by striking fjords and traditional rorbuer (fishermen's cabins).

- **Tromvik:** Located near Tromsø, Tromvik offers a tranquil and picturesque setting away from the city's hustle, allowing for an undisturbed Northern Lights experience.
- **Gjesvær:** This charming village on the island of Magerøya offers remote Arctic experiences, including birdwatching and authentic fishing culture, amidst the dance of the Northern Lights.

Norway is a magical land of Northern Lights, where travelers can witness the awe-inspiring beauty of the Aurora Borealis in some of the world's most stunning locations. From the vibrant city of Tromsø to the breathtaking North Cape and the tranquil Lofoten Islands, Norway offers numerous destinations to chase this celestial spectacle. Engaging in activities like dog sledding, snowmobiling, and ice fishing adds excitement to the journey. To capture the full grandeur of the Northern Lights, adventurers can explore hidden gems like Senja, Svalbard, Lyngen Alps, Hamnøy, Tromvik, and Gjesvær, where fewer crowds and unspoiled landscapes create a truly unforgettable experience. So, embark on a journey to Norway and let the Northern Lights weave their enchanting spell, illuminating the Arctic skies and captivating your soul.

## Bergen

Bergen is a vibrant city in Norway, known for its picturesque landscapes, rich history, and unique attractions. Here are some of the tourism highlights, activities, and hidden gems in Bergen:

- Bryggen: A UNESCO World Heritage Site, Bryggen is a historic wharf with colorful wooden buildings dating back to the Hanseatic era. It's a must-visit attraction that offers a glimpse into Bergen's trading history.[1]
- Fløibanen Funicular: Take a ride on the Fløibanen funicular to Mount Fløyen for breathtaking panoramic views of Bergen. Once at the top, enjoy hiking trails, a playground, and a café amidst stunning natural surroundings.
- Bergenhus Fortress: Explore the Bergenhus Fortress, one of the oldest and best-preserved fortresses in Norway. Discover its medieval halls, visit the Rosenkrantz Tower, and learn about Bergen's military history.
- Fish Market: Visit the lively Fish Market (Fisketorget) to experience the vibrant atmosphere and sample fresh seafood. It's a great place to try local delicacies like Bergen fish soup and Norwegian salmon.
- Mount Ulriken: Take a cable car or hike up Mount Ulriken, the highest of the Seven Mountains surrounding Bergen. Enjoy panoramic views of the city, go ziplining, or try paragliding for an adventurous experience.
- Gamlehaugen: Visit Gamlehaugen, the royal residence in Bergen, known for its beautiful architecture and stunning surroundings. Explore the park, stroll along the shoreline, and admire the castle-like mansion.

- Edvard Grieg's Home: Discover the former home of renowned composer Edvard Grieg at Troldhaugen. Explore the museum, visit Grieg's composer's cabin, and enjoy concerts showcasing his music in a picturesque setting.
- Bergen Maritime Museum: Delve into Bergen's maritime history at the Bergen Maritime Museum. Learn about the city's connection to the sea, explore exhibits on shipbuilding, navigation, and seafaring traditions.

### Hidden Gems:

- Stoltzekleiven: Challenge yourself with a hike up the steep Stoltzekleiven trail, which rewards you with stunning views of Bergen and the surrounding fjords. It's a local favorite for outdoor enthusiasts.
- VilVite Science Center: Engage in interactive exhibits and hands-on activities at VilVite Science Center. Perfect for families, this hidden gem offers educational fun for all ages.
- Lysøen Island: Take a boat trip to Lysøen Island and visit the villa of composer Ole Bull. The island offers serene landscapes, beautiful gardens, and a glimpse into the life of the famous musician.
- Fantoft Stave Church: Explore the Fantoft Stave Church, a replica of a medieval wooden church with intricate architecture. It's a hidden gem tucked away in a picturesque forested area.

## Lofoten

Lofoten, located in Norway, is a breathtaking archipelago known for its stunning landscapes, picturesque villages, and rich cultural heritage. Here are some of the tourism highlights, activities, and hidden gems that make Lofoten a must-visit destination:

- Scenic Beauty: Lofoten is famous for its dramatic landscapes characterized by soaring mountains, deep fjords, pristine beaches, and crystal-clear waters. The towering peaks, such as the iconic Reinebringen, offer breathtaking panoramic views that are perfect for photography and hiking.

- Fishing Villages: Explore the charming fishing villages scattered across the archipelago, including Reine, Hamnøy, Nusfjord, and Henningsvær. These villages are known for their colorful wooden houses, vibrant harbors, and authentic fishing culture. Stroll through the narrow streets, visit local galleries, and experience the traditional way of life.

- Northern Lights: Lofoten is a fantastic destination to witness the mesmerizing Northern Lights (Aurora Borealis). The dark, unpolluted skies and the aurora's dancing colors create a truly magical experience. Winter months, from September to April, offer the best chances to witness this natural phenomenon.

- Wildlife Watching: Lofoten is teeming with wildlife. Take a boat tour or join a sea safari to spot majestic sea eagles, puffins, seals, and whales. The archipelago's waters are home to various marine species, making it a paradise for nature enthusiasts.

- Outdoor Activities: Engage in a range of outdoor activities that take advantage of Lofoten's stunning natural surroundings. Enjoy hiking along scenic trails, go kayaking through the fjords, try your hand at fishing, or embark on a cycling adventure along the picturesque routes.

- Beaches: Despite its northern location, Lofoten boasts beautiful white sandy beaches. Utakleiv, Haukland, and Kvalvika beaches are among the most popular ones. These beaches offer a unique contrast between the turquoise waters and the surrounding mountains, making them ideal spots for relaxation and photography.

- Viking Heritage: Delve into the Viking history and visit sites like the Lofotr Viking Museum in Borg. Experience the daily life of Vikings, explore the reconstructed Chieftain's house, and participate in interactive exhibits that provide insights into their fascinating culture.

- Rorbu Experience: Stay in traditional fisherman's cabins known as "rorbuer." These cozy cabins provide an authentic and comfortable accommodation option. Wake up to stunning views of the sea, immerse yourself in the local atmosphere, and enjoy fresh seafood delicacies.

- Arts and Culture: Lofoten has a vibrant arts and cultural scene. Visit art galleries and studios to appreciate the works of local artists inspired by the stunning surroundings. Attend traditional music festivals and cultural events to experience the region's rich heritage.

- Hidden Gems: Explore the lesser-known gems of Lofoten, such as the remote beaches of Bunes and Horseid, the hidden cove of Kvalvika, or the charming village of Å (pronounced "oh"). These off-the-beaten-path destinations offer tranquility and a chance to connect with nature.

Lofoten's unique blend of natural beauty, cultural heritage, and outdoor activities makes it an unforgettable destination for travelers seeking adventure, relaxation, and immersion in Norway's stunning landscapes

## Tromso.

Tromsø, located in Norway, is a captivating destination known for its stunning natural beauty and unique experiences. Here are some tourism highlights, activities, and hidden gems to explore in Tromsø:

- Tromsø Bridge: Take a stroll on the iconic Tromsø Bridge, which connects the mainland to Tromsøya Island. Enjoy panoramic views of the city, fjords, and mountains as you walk or cycle across this architectural marvel.
- Tromsø Cathedral: Visit the Tromsø Cathedral, also known as the Arctic Cathedral, with its striking modern design and iconic triangular shape. Admire the stunning stained glass windows and attend a concert to experience the exceptional acoustics of this remarkable church.
- Polaria: Explore Polaria, an Arctic-themed experience center that offers interactive exhibits on the region's unique wildlife, climate, and culture. Enjoy fascinating presentations, visit the aquarium,

and witness feeding sessions with adorable seals.

- Tromsø University Museum: Discover the rich natural and cultural history of the Arctic at the Tromsø University Museum. Learn about the region's indigenous Sami people, explore exhibits on Arctic ecosystems, and delve into the fascinating world of polar research.

- Fjellheisen Cable Car: Take a ride on the Fjellheisen Cable Car to the top of Mount Storsteinen. Enjoy breathtaking panoramic views of Tromsø, its surrounding islands, and the majestic mountains. Indulge in a delicious meal at the mountaintop restaurant while savoring the stunning scenery.

- Arctic-Alpine Botanic Garden: Explore the northernmost botanical garden in the world, the Arctic-Alpine Botanic Garden. Wander through the beautiful displays of Arctic and alpine plants, learn about their adaptations, and enjoy the serene atmosphere of this unique garden.

- Sami Culture: Immerse yourself in the indigenous Sami culture by visiting the Sami Center in Tromsø. Learn about their traditional way of life, experience reindeer sledding, try Sami cuisine, and listen to captivating stories and joik (traditional Sami songs).

- Arctic Wildlife: Tromsø offers opportunities for wildlife enthusiasts to spot a variety of Arctic animals. Join a guided tour to observe whales, seals, seabirds, and other fascinating marine life in their natural habitat.

- Midnight Sun: During the summer months, experience the phenomenon of the Midnight Sun in Tromsø. Enjoy extended daylight hours and engage in activities such as hiking, fishing, and kayaking under the magical glow of the sun even at midnight.

## Trondheim

Trondheim, located in Norway, is a vibrant city with a rich history and plenty of tourism highlights, activities, and hidden gems to explore. Here's a description of Trondheim, citing its popular attractions, activities, and hidden gems:

- Nidaros Cathedral: Nidaros Cathedral is the largest medieval building in Scandinavia and a significant pilgrimage site. This magnificent Gothic cathedral is known for its intricate architecture, stunning stained glass windows, and historical importance as the coronation church of Norwegian kings.
- Trondheim Old Town: Take a stroll through the charming streets of Trondheim's Old Town, known as Bakklandet. Admire the colorful wooden houses, quaint cafés, and boutique shops. It's a picturesque area with a unique atmosphere, especially along the iconic street of Gamle Bybro (Old Town Bridge).
- Kristiansten Fortress: Situated on a hill overlooking the city, Kristiansten Fortress offers panoramic views of Trondheim. Explore the fort's historical grounds, visit the museum inside, and enjoy a peaceful walk in the surrounding park.
- Ringve Museum: Music enthusiasts will appreciate a visit to Ringve Museum, which showcases a vast collection of musical instruments from different eras. The museum also features

beautiful gardens and offers concerts during the summer months.

- Rockheim: For music lovers interested in contemporary Norwegian music history, Rockheim is a must-visit. This interactive museum explores the country's popular music culture and its impact on society.

- Trondheim Science Center: Perfect for families and curious minds, the Trondheim Science Center provides hands-on exhibits and interactive displays focused on science, technology, and mathematics. It's an engaging and educational experience for visitors of all ages.

- Solsiden: Solsiden is a lively waterfront district known for its restaurants, bars, and shopping opportunities. Enjoy a meal at one of the many eateries, relax by the water, or explore the trendy shops in this vibrant area.

Hidden Gems:

- Bymarka: Escape the city and venture into Bymarka, a vast forested area surrounding Trondheim. It offers numerous hiking trails, serene lakes, and breathtaking viewpoints. Bymarka is a true hidden gem for outdoor enthusiasts and nature lovers.

- Munkholmen: Take a short boat trip to Munkholmen, a small island with a fascinating history. It was once a medieval monastery and later served as a prison. Today, visitors can explore the ruins, enjoy the beach, or simply relax in this tranquil setting.

- Fosen Peninsula: Embark on a scenic drive along the Fosen

Peninsula, located just outside Trondheim. This picturesque area features idyllic coastal landscapes, charming villages, and opportunities for fishing, hiking, and wildlife spotting.

- Sverresborg Trøndelag Folk Museum: Step back in time at Sverresborg Trøndelag Folk Museum, an open-air museum showcasing traditional Norwegian buildings and cultural heritage. Explore the historical structures and gain insights into Trondheim's past.

## The Stave Churches

Norway's stave churches hold a significant place in the country's cultural and architectural heritage. These remarkable wooden structures date back to the medieval era, showcasing exceptional craftsmanship and design. The term "stave" refers to the load-bearing wooden posts used in their construction, which gives them their distinctive name. These churches are not only places of worship but also popular tourist attractions, offering visitors a glimpse into Norway's rich history and traditional building techniques.

### Historical Significance and Architecture

Stave churches first emerged in Norway during the early Middle Ages, with the oldest surviving example being Urnes Stave Church, built around 1130 and designated as a UNESCO World Heritage Site. These churches served as vital centers of religious and social life for local communities. Their construction typically utilized a wooden framework with intricate carvings and decorative elements, often depicting scenes from Norse mythology, Christian symbols, and traditional folklore.

**Tourist Highlights: Where to Experience Stave Churches**

Tourists exploring Norway have several opportunities to experience these captivating stave churches. Some of the most renowned and accessible ones are:

1. **Urnes Stave Church:** Located in the Sogn og Fjordane region, Urnes Stave Church is a UNESCO-listed site and exemplifies the iconic Urnes style, characterized by its elegantly interwoven dragon motifs.
2. **Borgund Stave Church:** Situated in Laerdal, Sogn og Fjordane, this church is one of the best-preserved examples, showcasing intricate woodcarvings and a distinct black color due to tar-coated exteriors.
3. **Heddal Stave Church:** The largest stave church in Norway may be found at Notodden, Telemark. It is divided into three portions with various architectural styles.
4. **Gol Stave Church:** Located in Gol, Buskerud, this church exhibits both Christian and Norse influences, with unique dragon carvings and an ancient history.

**Tourist Activities: Exploring the Heritage**

Visiting these stave churches offers tourists a chance to explore the historical and architectural heritage of Norway. Some popular tourist activities include:

1. **Guided Tours:** Engaging in guided tours enhances the experience, as knowledgeable guides share the fascinating stories and legends surrounding these ancient structures.
2. **Photography:** The intricate woodcarvings, distinctive architecture, and scenic surroundings provide excellent photography opportunities.
3. **Cultural Events:** Some stave churches host cultural events, such as traditional concerts or local festivals, allowing tourists to immerse themselves in Norway's vibrant cultural scene.
4. **Nature Excursions:** Many stave churches are situated amidst breathtaking landscapes, making them ideal starting points for nature excursions and hikes.

**Hidden Gems: Lesser-Known Stave Churches**

While the well-known stave churches attract a significant number of tourists, several lesser-known gems also deserve exploration:

1. **Kaupanger Stave Church:** Located near Sogndal in Sogn og Fjordane, this church boasts beautiful carvings and an intimate atmosphere.
2. **Torpo Stave Church:** Situated in Ål, Buskerud, this church offers a tranquil setting and a chance to escape the crowds.
3. **Eidsborg Stave Church:** Nestled in Tokke, Telemark, this small

and charming church is known for its peaceful surroundings.

Norway's stave churches represent a unique blend of history, culture, and architectural prowess. Tourists visiting these remarkable wooden structures can immerse themselves in the country's rich heritage while enjoying the natural beauty that surrounds them. From the well-known attractions to the hidden gems, the stave churches of Norway offer an unforgettable experience that brings the past to life, making them an essential part of any traveler's itinerary in this enchanting Scandinavian nation.

1. **If you haven't already done so, scan the QR code at the beginning of the book** and download THE SPECIALIZED TRIPS AND UNIQUE EXPERIENCES IN NORWAY IN OUR EBOOK
2. **Scan the QR code below and <u>leave quick feedback on Amazon!</u>**

# SCAN ME

# Chapter 3:

# Outdoor Experiences and Activities

Norway offers an outdoor playground that beckons travelers to embark on unforgettable experiences. From the thrill-seekers to the nature lovers, this Scandinavian gem has something for everyone to revel in its pristine beauty.

In Norway, the great outdoors unfolds like a tapestry of wonders, inviting visitors to immerse themselves in its breathtaking splendor. Whether you seek adrenaline-pumping adventures or peaceful encounters with nature, the country's diverse topography caters to all interests and aspirations.

Majestic fjords such as Geirangerfjord and Nærøyfjord boast an otherworldly beauty, and exploring them on cruises, hikes, or kayaking tours unveils nature's grandeur in its purest form.

For those yearning to experience Norway's iconic landscapes in a more organized manner, Norway in a Nutshell presents an all-encompassing tour combining a ferry ride through Naeroyfjord with the scenic Flåm railway. This packaged tour showcases the best of Norway's fjords and mountain vistas in a single, convenient journey.

Nature enthusiasts can challenge themselves with exhilarating hikes, such as the iconic Trolltunga, offering the perfect backdrop for creative photography and unforgettable memories. Bryggen in Bergen, a UNESCO World Heritage Site, unveils the country's historic charm, showcasing colorful Hanseatic Houses that have stood the test of time.

But Norway's allure extends beyond its fjords and historic landmarks. Adventure seekers can traverse the Lofoten Islands on an unforgettable road trip, while winter enthusiasts can delight in skiing escapades amidst captivating mountain scenery.

Norway's outdoor activities cater to all tastes, from the thrill of kayaking on the Geirangerfjord to embracing the romance of a getaway for two. The country's commitment to sustainability ensures that visitors can enjoy its natural wonders responsibly, with many eco-certified destinations to explore.

Whether you're a seasoned adventurer or an explorer looking to unwind, Norway's outdoor offerings promise an extraordinary journey filled with unforgettable moments. So, gear up and get ready to embrace the great outdoors in Norway – a land of endless wonders and cherished memories awaiting your discovery.

## Hiking in Norwegian National Parks: Discovering Pristine Wilderness

Norway's diverse landscape, with its 47 national parks, towering mountains, extensive coastline, and famous fjords, provides an exceptional backdrop for hiking enthusiasts. Hiking is deeply ingrained in the Norwegian lifestyle, with locals embracing "friluftsliv," an outdoors lifestyle, year-round. During the summer and fall, hiking becomes especially popular, and numerous marked trails criss-cross the country, leading hikers through breathtaking wilderness and offering a chance to connect with nature.

### *Famous Hiking Trails in Norway*

- **Preikestolen (Pulpit Rock):** One of Norway's most well-known hikes is Preikestolen, which is close to the Lysefjord and is famed for its breathtaking fjord vistas. Hikers reach a clifftop that towers over 1,600 feet above the fjord after a four-hour roundtrip climb, offering a spectacular vantage point for stunning sights.
- **Kjeragbolten:** This climb goes to a glacial rock jammed in a mountain crevice with a view of the Lysefjord and provides an

exhilarating photo opportunity. The challenging 7-mile roundtrip hike, which takes around 8 hours to complete and has an elevation rise of more than 1,800 feet, is appropriate for experienced hikers.

- **Trolltunga (The Troll's Tongue):** Trolltunga, a well-known destination trek because of its distinctive rock formation, frequently draws long lines of hikers anxious to take the famous snapshot of a lone hiker on the unusual rock more than 2,300 feet above Lake Ringedalsvatnet. It takes 10 to 12 hours to do the strenuous 17-mile roundtrip climb, or 7-9 hours to complete an alternate 12.5-mile route.

- **Besseggen:** Besseggen is recognized for its exceptional lake view and is located in the Jotunheimen National Park, which is home to Norway's tallest mountains. On one side of the slope, hikers can admire the blue Bessvatnet lake and on the other, the green Gjene lake. It takes 6 to 8 hours roundtrip to do this walk, which National Geographic named one of the top 20 most thrilling in the world.

- **Romsdalseggen:** This trail, which is found in Andalsnes, provides stunning views of the Romsdalsfjord, the Romsdal Alps, and the surrounding area. The walk is appropriate for experienced hikers and lasts between 10 to 12 hours.

### *Hiking Trails Near Oslo*

Oslo, the capital city of Norway, also offers an array of easily accessible hiking trails through its efficient T-Bane metro system. Some of the best hiking trails near Oslo include:

- **Østmarka:** Located in the northwestern corner of the Østmarka forest, this hiking trail offers a picturesque route from Ellingsrudåsen to Mariholtet Sportsstue, passing alongside the beautiful Nord Elvåga lake.

- **Nordmarka: Skjennungstua:** North of Oslo, the Nordmarka region offers a well-signposted hiking trail from Frognerseteren to Skjennungstua, where hikers can enjoy a log cabin cafe with stunning views of the forest.

- **Kolsåstoppen:** Accessible via Metro line 3 to Kolsås, this trail leads to the prominent Kolsåstoppen ridge, offering excellent views across Oslo. The nature reserve in this region is also popular for rock climbing.

Hiking in Norwegian national parks and near Oslo provides a unique opportunity to discover pristine wilderness and embrace the country's friluftsliv lifestyle. From famous trails with unforgettable views to easily accessible routes via the Oslo metro system, Norway offers a hiker's paradise with breathtaking landscapes, diverse flora and fauna, and a chance to connect with nature in its purest form

## Kayaking and Canoeing: Paddling Through Serene Fjords and Lakes

Norway, with its stunning coastline, majestic fjords, serene lakes, and picturesque islands, offers a paradise for kayaking and canoeing enthusiasts. The country's pristine waters, surrounded by breathtaking landscapes, provide an unparalleled experience for tourists seeking to explore the beauty of nature from the water. From the southern coastal towns to the Arctic reaches of the north, Norway presents a diverse range of paddling opportunities that cater to both beginners and experienced paddlers. In this thorough tour, we'll examine some of Norway's most well-liked kayaking and canoeing spots, emphasizing the unforgettable experiences that await visitors.

### Southern Norway: Canoeing and Kayaking in the Archipelago

Southern Norway, with its charming towns, vibrant harbors, and thousands of islands, offers a dreamlike setting for paddlers. Kayaking and canoeing along the southern coastline provide an opportunity to immerse oneself in the serene beauty of the archipelago. Cities like Kristiansand, Arendal, Grimstad, Lillesand, and Mandal serve as ideal starting points for explorations in this region.

Guided tours and professional guides are recommended to ensure safety and to make the most of the experience. Paddlers can navigate through sheltered waters, discover hidden coves, and witness the coastal culture that thrives in this picturesque region. The archipelago's calm waters and scenic vistas provide a perfect backdrop for capturing memorable moments with a waterproof camera.

### Fjord Norway: Immersive Kayaking in World-Famous Fjords

Fjord Norway presents a kayaker's paradise with its renowned fjords, dramatic mountains, and pristine glacial lakes. For a truly immersive experience, joining a guided kayak tour is highly recommended. Paddling on the sparkling waters of the Sognefjord, Hardangerfjord, Geirangerfjord, and Nærøyfjord surrounded by majestic mountains is an unforgettable adventure.

Guided tours cater to both beginners and experienced paddlers, ensuring everyone can explore these natural wonders safely. Navigating through the deep fjords, paddlers can witness breathtaking waterfalls cascading down the cliffs, explore small idyllic islands, and absorb the tranquility of the UNESCO-protected fjords. Additionally, glacial lakes like Jostedalen, with its connection to the Nigardsbreen glacier, offer a unique starting point for a glacier adventure with guides to ensure safety.

### *Northern Norway: Paddling Through Remote Beauty*

Northern Norway offers a once-in-a-lifetime kayaking adventure with its lonely fishing settlements, rough coastlines, and breathtaking beaches. Even while the entire Northern Norwegian coast offers excellent paddling locations, areas like Lofoten, Vesterlen, and Senja stand out for their breathtaking beauty.

Guided tours are crucial in this area due to the occasionally rough conditions and cold waters. Paddling along the fjords and exploring the unique landscapes is a remarkable way to witness the unspoiled beauty of this Arctic region. From the tranquility of remote islands to the grandeur of towering peaks, Northern Norway rewards kayakers with unforgettable moments in nature.

### *Helgeland Coast: Sea Kayaking in a Scenic Wonder*

Located just south of the Arctic Circle, the Helgeland coast is renowned for being one of Norway's best areas for sea kayaking. This region offers a perfect blend of sea kayaking, traditional rorbu stays (fishermen's cabins), and delectable local culinary experiences.

Paddlers can explore charming islands like Dønna, Træna, and the UNESCO-protected islands of Vega, all while basking in the stunning coastal landscape. Guided tours ensure that visitors get the most out of this coastal paradise, allowing them to relax on pristine beaches, encounter diverse wildlife, and connect with the region's rich maritime heritage.

### *Canoeing and Kayaking on Canals: An Idyllic Journey*

Paddling on Norway's canals offers a unique and fascinating experience. The Halden Canal and the Telemark Canal in Eastern Norway are particularly popular destinations for such journeys. Kayakers can revel in the beauty of the landscape and admire the stunning locks along the canals.

Combining paddling on the canal with a boat trip further enhances the experience. Many canal boats allow canoes and kayaks onboard, offering a convenient way to explore these historic waterways.

### *City Kayaking: Exploring Urban Waters*

For a different perspective on Norway's cities, city kayaking offers a refreshing alternative to sightseeing buses. Paddling through the heart of cities like Oslo and Bergen, tourists can admire iconic landmarks, waterfront architecture, and vibrant city life from the water.

Guided city kayaking tours provide insights into the urban history and cultural heritage of these cities, offering a unique blend of outdoor adventure and urban exploration.

## Glacier Exploration: Witnessing Ice Giants Up Close

Norway's diverse and stunning landscapes are not only known for its majestic fjords and towering mountains but also for its awe-inspiring glaciers. With over 2,500 glaciers throughout the country, Norway offers a plethora of opportunities for tourists to witness these frozen giants up close. From the Arctic Svalbard archipelago to the mainland's Southern and Northern regions, each glacier presents a unique experience for travelers seeking to explore the beauty and power of ice formations. In this comprehensive guide, we will delve into some of Norway's most remarkable glaciers, how to access them, and the importance of preserving these natural wonders.

### *Jostedalsbreen: The Largest Glacier in Continental Europe*

Located in Fjord Norway, Jostedalsbreen is not only the largest glacier in Norway but also the largest in continental Europe. Covering an area of 474 square kilometers, this temperate glacier offers various activities for tourists throughout the year. Summer skiing, hiking, snowshoeing, and ice climbing are popular pursuits for adventurers seeking to experience the breathtaking beauty of Jostedalsbreen. The glacier has many branches, with Nigardsbreen being one of the most accessible and famous ones.

Visitors can hike, take a boat trip, or even paddle on the emerald green glacier waters in a kayak for a unique and immersive experience. However, it is essential to engage in guided tours led by experienced professionals and equipped with proper safety gear to ensure a safe exploration of the glacier's ice walls and crevasses.

### *Nigardsbreen: A Fascinating Offshoot of Jostedalsbreen*

As an offshoot of the massive Jostedalsbreen, Nigardsbreen, located in Western Norway, offers an excellent opportunity to explore blue ice crevasses and towering frozen towers. Glacier hikes, accompanied by local guides, provide a thrilling adventure for both seasoned hikers and families with kids. The Nigardsbreen Glacier Centre in Sogndal serves as a starting point for visitors to access the glacier.

To reach Nigardsbreen, tourists can start their journey in the coastal city of Bergen and take an express boat up the coast to Sogndal. From there, buses operate to the Breheimsenteret Glacier Centre from the end of June until the end of August. From Breheimsenteret, visitors can either hike for approximately 45 minutes to reach the glacier or opt for a boat trip along the Jostedøla river.

## *Svartisen: A Majestic Glacier in Northern Norway*

Located in the far north of Norway, Svartisen is the country's second-largest glacier, surrounded by steep mountain slopes and a crystal-clear lake. Set within the Svartisen-Saltfjellet National Park, this untouched wilderness within the Arctic Circle offers stunning views of the massive ice cap.

Travelers can savor the majestic scenery from the nearby Brestua restaurant, where they can enjoy warming Norwegian dishes and visit a small museum dedicated to Svartisen and its famous visitors. Access to Svartisen usually begins in the town of Bodø, which can be reached by plane from Oslo or Trondheim. From Bodø, a scenic drive along the Fv17 road takes visitors to Holandsvika, where a boat service operates during the summer months to cross the Holand Fjord.

## *Briksdalsbreen: A Frozen Waterfall at the End of Oldedalen Valley*

Briksdalsbreen, another arm of the Jostedalsbreen glacier, is situated within the Jostedalsbreen National Park. Characterized by high mountains, peaceful fjords, and picturesque hiking trails, this region offers an unforgettable experience for nature enthusiasts.

At the end of the Oldedalen valley, Briksdalsbreen cascades down the mountainside like a colossal frozen waterfall. Travelers can choose to walk the 3-kilometer route from the Briksdalsbre Mountain Lodge to the glacier or take a ride on old-fashioned "troll cars" for a more comfortable journey.

*Preserving Norway's Glaciers for Future Generations*

While Norway's glaciers offer stunning landscapes and thrilling adventures for tourists, it is essential to recognize the impacts of climate change on these ice formations. Global warming poses a significant threat to the country's glaciers, leading to rapid melting and alterations in their appearance.

Preserving these natural wonders for future generations is a responsibility that falls upon everyone, from policymakers to individual travelers. Encouraging sustainable tourism practices, supporting conservation efforts, and raising awareness about climate change are vital steps to safeguard Norway's glaciers for the years to come.

## Fjord Cruises: Navigating Through Nature's Masterpieces

Norway's fjords are nature's masterpieces, captivating tourists with their breathtaking beauty and serene landscapes. Fjord cruises offer a unique and immersive experience, allowing travelers to navigate through these awe-inspiring creations while witnessing cascading waterfalls, majestic mountains, and picturesque villages. This comprehensive guide explores some of the best fjord cruises in Norway, providing travelers with a glimpse of the stunning scenery and memorable adventures that await them.

### *Lysefjord and Preikestolen Cruise from Stavanger*

This fjord trip departs from Stavanger and takes visitors to the well-known

Lysefjord where they may take in the majestic Preikestolen (Pulpit Rock) from the water. The trip provides chances to see the mysterious Vagabonds Cave and see adorable goats grazing in summer pastures. No matter the weather, the breathtaking Hengjane waterfalls' cool spray will provide travelers with an amazing experience. Visitors looking to explore the splendor of the Lysefjord and its environs can take catamaran cruises aboard contemporary, cozy vessels out of Rdne and Go Fjords with confidence.

## *Flørli 4444: Exploring the Hengjane Falls and World-Record Wooden Staircase*

This daring cruise ventures into Lysefjord and brings passengers to Flrli, a hamlet noted for its 4,444-step wooden stairway that holds the world record. Visitors can climb the stairs to the former power plant, which is 750 meters above the village, as part of the tour and take in the breathtaking scenery along the route. A special chance to combine fjord exploration with a strenuous and gratifying walk is provided by the Flrli 4444 cruise.

## *Ålesund to Geiranger: A Journey Through Three Fjords*

This exciting trip departs from Lesund and travels through three distinct fjords, exhibiting the spectacular grandeur of the Norwegian landscape.

After exploring the renowned Geirangerfjord, visitors have the option of staying in Geiranger or taking a boat back to shore. On the ship, you can have lunch and go on a quick sightseeing excursion to the closest lookout points at rnesvingen (the Eagle curve) or Flydalsjuvet. Tourists will remember this voyage for seeing the magnificent Brudeslret waterfall and the abandoned farms clinging to the mountain walls.

### *Flåm - Gudvangen - Flåm: Discovering the Nærøyfjord*

On this fjord trip, see the Nryfjord, the Sognefjord's narrowest and most magnificent inlet. Travelers set sail over the picturesque Aurlandsfjord, listed as a UNESCO World Heritage Site, from either Flm or Gudvangen. The vessel then travels through the Nryfjord until it reaches Gudvangen, which is tucked away in the small fjord's center. The trek, which lasts around two hours one way and provides breathtaking vistas of this amazing natural beauty.

### *Norwegian Coastal Express: The Original Coastal Voyage*

Celebrating 130 years of being Norway's coastal lifeline, the Norwegian Coastal Express offers an unrivaled fjord cruise experience. Known as "The World's Most Beautiful Voyage," this iconic journey, loved since 1893, allows travelers to explore the stunning Norwegian fjords, including the country's second-largest fjord, Hardangerfjord. The UNESCO World Heritage Site, Geirangerfjord, is often referred to as the "crown jewel" of Norwegian fjords. For a more off-the-beaten-path experience, the neighboring Hjørundfjord captivates with activities such as fjord fishing and kayaking. The cruise also offers opportunities to explore the rich history, culture, and beauty of Norway's cities and villages, making it a must-do for any traveler seeking an unforgettable fjord cruise experience

## Skiing and Snowboarding: Thrilling Adventures on Norway's Slopes

When it comes to winter adventures, Norway stands as a premier destination for skiing and snowboarding enthusiasts. With its stunning mountains, glaciers, and fjords, Norway offers a unique and captivating experience for skiers and snowboarders alike. This comprehensive guide explores the thrilling adventures that await tourists on Norway's slopes, highlighting the country's best ski resorts and the wide range of activities for families, beginners, intermediates, and advanced skiers.

### *Skiing in Norway: A Winter Wonderland*

Norway's ski resorts offer guests an incredible winter wonderland experience with their vast and quiet pistes. The country's success in the Winter Olympics is a testament to the superb skiing conditions it offers. Unlike its Alpine counterparts, Norwegian ski resorts provide peaceful and uncrowded mountains, complemented by state-of-the-art lift systems. Travelers can explore gentle slopes suitable for beginners and intermediates, as well as challenging off-piste terrains for advanced skiers. With breathtaking views of fjords and frozen lakes, skiing in Norway offers an unforgettable and magical experience.

### Ski Resorts in Norway: The Best Picks

Norway boasts over 120 ski resorts, each offering a unique and exhilarating skiing experience. Some of the best ski resorts in Norway include:

- Myrkdalen, Voss: An ideal spot for families with 22 ski trails catering to all levels, from beginners to cross-country skiers. This resort, with an annual snowfall of around five meters, promises an authentic Norwegian experience amidst valleys and fjords.
- Trysil, Osterdalen: Norway's largest ski resort, boasting 69 slopes, 32 lifts, and over 100km of cross-country ski trails. Night skiing and family-friendly amenities make Trysil a top choice for all ski enthusiasts.
- Hemsedal, Hallingdal: Located in Southern Norway, Hemsedal offers plentiful snow coverage from November to May, making it an attractive destination for skiing. With 53 slopes, 21 ski lifts, and dedicated areas for children, Hemsedal provides a fantastic skiing experience.

### Skiing Activities and Off-Piste Adventures

Norway's ski resorts offer a wide range of activities beyond skiing and snowboarding. Families can enjoy dog sledding, horse-drawn sleigh rides, and night skiing. Cross-country skiing holds a special place in Norway's culture and is a popular activity. Après-ski is a laid-back affair, with cozy bars and restaurants offering local cuisine in front of log fires. Don't miss the chance to sample Akevitt, the local tipple, adding a touch of Norwegian tradition to your winter adventure.

## *Ski Touring with Norway Mountain Guides*

For the adventurous souls seeking untouched territory, ski touring with Norway Mountain Guides offers a unique and unforgettable experience. Explore majestic landscapes, trek through unbroken snow, and breathe in the fresh mountain air while combining the beauty of fjords and skiing in one trip. Guided tours take visitors to peaks and off-piste areas suitable for both experienced skiers and beginners. The focus on safe trips and untouched snow ensures an extraordinary ski touring adventure outside Bergen, including areas like Voss, Myrkdalen, Nærøyfjorden, Kvamskogen, and the Hardanger Fjord. Skiers are guaranteed to witness Norway's natural beauty and enjoy a memorable skiing experience with the guidance of local experts.

## Fishing and Wildlife Safaris: Immersing in Norway's Natural Abundance

Norway's natural abundance, from its majestic fjords to its diverse wildlife, makes it an ideal destination for fishing and wildlife safaris. With its pristine landscapes, rich marine life, and opportunities to spot iconic Arctic creatures, tourists can immerse themselves in the wonders of Norway's wilderness. This comprehensive guide explores the thrilling fishing and wildlife safari experiences that await tourists in Norway, highlighting popular tours and destinations where visitors can get up close with the country's unique flora and fauna.

## *Wildlife Safaris in Norway: Exploring Arctic Wonders*

Norway offers a range of wildlife safari tours that allow travelers to experience the Arctic wonders up close. Some of the most amazing wildlife safaris in Norway include:

- Cruise along Spitsbergen's coast, ice edge, and inner fjords while photographing renowned Arctic animals including polar bears, seabirds, and more on the 14-day itinerary aboard the Ultramarine. During your expedition, you can pick up shooting tips from professionals and take advantage of the Arctic summer's nonstop daylight.
- Fjords of Norway and Svalbard, the Arctic (16-day itinerary on the National Geographic Resolution): Visit the Lofoten Islands, paddle in deep fjords, and explore Norway's northern fjords. This journey allows visitors to experience the ice and wildness of the Svalbard archipelago while maintaining a balance between picturesque appeal and stunning wilderness.
- Take a voyage through North Spitsbergen to see stunning landscapes and countless seabirds. North Spitsbergen, In Search of Polar Bear & Pack Ice (8-day Itinerary Aboard MV Hondius).

The possibility to see polar bears as they roam the Hinlopen Strait and St. Johns Fjord locations is the highlight of this trip.

- Highlights of Svalbard: Travel along the west coast of Spitsbergen via pack ice up to 80°N. In the midst of icebergs and Arctic tundra, this experience offers frequent wildlife interactions and plenty of chances to see iconic Arctic wildlife, including polar bears.

- Discover the remote islands and fjords of northern Norway, including the high Arctic archipelago of Svalbard, on the 10-day itinerary onboard the National Geographic Endurance. This voyage enables participants to observe the cycles of nature while looking for walruses, seals, and other Arctic species.

### *Wildlife Sea Safari: Fjord Norway's Coastal Adventure*

Along Norway's picturesque fjords and coastline, tourists can embark on exciting Wildlife Sea Safaris. One such safari offered by 62°NORD takes participants on a thrilling two-hour ride along the coastline outside Ålesund in a high-speed RIB-boat. The tour typically includes visits to seal colonies and Runde's famous bird colonies, where eagles and puffins can be observed. The safari also passes by small coastal communities, providing a glimpse of local life and culture. This adventure promises action-packed moments and breathtaking views of Norway's marine and avian life, making it a memorable experience for wildlife enthusiasts.

### *Fishing in Norway: A Paradise for Anglers*

For fishing enthusiasts, Norway is a paradise with its abundant rivers, lakes, and fjords teeming with fish. The country offers numerous opportunities for recreational fishing, and tourists can experience different types of fishing, including sea fishing, fly fishing, and ice fishing. Some of the popular fishing destinations in Norway include:

- Lofoten Islands: Known for its dramatic landscapes and rich marine life, Lofoten Islands offer excellent fishing opportunities, especially for catching cod, halibut, and salmon.
- North Cape: Located in the northernmost part of mainland Norway, North Cape is famous for its scenic beauty and fantastic sea fishing. Anglers can catch species like cod, haddock, and redfish.
- Tromsø: As a vibrant city surrounded by stunning fjords and mountains, Tromsø offers fantastic fishing experiences, both in the sea and on freshwater rivers and lakes.
- Sognefjord: The longest fjord in Norway, Sognefjord, offers diverse fishing experiences, including sea fishing for cod and mackerel, and freshwater fishing for salmon and trout.

# Chapter 4:
# Norwegian Culture and Traditions

**Unveiling Norwegian History: From Vikings to Modern Times**

Norwegian history is a fascinating journey that spans from the age of Vikings to modern times, leaving behind a rich legacy of cultural, political, and artistic influence. The Vikings, known for their maritime prowess and exploration, played a significant role in shaping Northern Europe and beyond. Today, their heritage, along with the Scandinavian countries they helped establish, continues to captivate the popular imagination through books, films, podcasts, and websites. This comprehensive discussion delves into what tourists need to know about Norway's captivating past, from the Viking era to its lasting influence on modern culture and society.

### The Viking Age: Warriors, Traders, and Explorers

The Viking Age began in the late 8th century (around 793 CE) with the first recorded Viking raid on the Lindisfarne monastery in England. The Vikings were not only warriors and raiders but also skilled traders, farmers, and shipbuilders. Their longships, fast-moving vessels, played a crucial role in their cultural coherence and unifying Norse tribes into a state.

The Vikings' influence extended far and wide, as they embarked on expeditions across Europe and beyond, engaging in trade, colonization, and conquest. They navigated the Baltic and North Seas, reaching as far as the Black Sea, Caspian Sea, Greenland, and North America, five centuries before Christopher Columbus. Viking colonizers founded cities and colonies such as Dublin in Ireland, Normandy in France, and Iceland, which became a springboard for the colonization of Greenland.

Despite their reputation for plundering, the Vikings also lived peacefully as traders and farmers, contributing to cultural exchange and economic growth. Their influence went beyond their time, as Norse sagas and mythology continue to inspire art, literature, and popular culture to this day.

### Preserving Viking Heritage: Oseberg and Gokstad Longships

Norway's Viking legacy remains tangible through the preservation of cultural treasures like the Oseberg and Gokstad longships. These historic longships survived sea voyages and were interred in burial mounds alongside dignitaries and valuable objects. Although excavated, restored, and displayed in the Viking Ship Museum in Oslo, the preservation of these ships faces challenges due to surging tourist numbers, leading to dust, vibrations, and temperature fluctuations that threaten the delicate wood.

To protect these unique artifacts, the Norwegian government has allocated around $200 million to build a new home for the ships, including a delicate operation to move them about 50 yards. The construction is expected to begin around 2021 and last for approximately five years.

The Viking ships, including the 70-foot Oseberg and 78-foot Gokstad, hold immense historical and cultural significance. They are evidence of the Vikings' maritime expertise and their ability to influence European societies of their time. These ships serve as a testament to the Vikings' skill as shipbuilders and explorers, leaving a lasting legacy that continues to captivate the world.

### *Cultural Legacy: Scandinavian Nations and Norse Sagas*

One of the greatest cultural legacies that the Vikings left behind is the formation of the sovereign Scandinavian countries of Denmark, Norway, and Sweden. Before the Viking Age, the Scandinavian peninsula consisted of fragmentary cultures and societies. However, the Vikings' activities, including raids, trading, and colonization, accelerated the formation of unified medieval kingdoms. The influx of resources and people transformed small trading communities into international centers of commerce, like Hedeby and Birka, with diverse populations.

Norse sagas, a collection of stories and histories compiled during the Viking Age, are another invaluable Viking legacy. These sagas cover a wide range of subjects, from family dramas to accounts of early Viking rulers. They offer insights into the Vikings' storytelling prowess and their rich mythology, cosmogony, and pantheon of gods.

The impact of Viking storytelling transcends time and has influenced modern popular culture and literature. Authors like C.S. Lewis and J.R.R. Tolkien drew inspiration from Norse sagas for their own epic tales, such as "The Chronicles of Narnia" and "The Lord of the Rings."

### *Modern-day Viking Influence*

The Vikings' legacy remains alive and well in modern Scandinavian culture and society. Scandinavian countries continue to embrace their Viking heritage, celebrating it through festivals, museums, and cultural events. Visitors to these countries can experience Viking-themed attractions and immerse themselves in the rich historical tapestry of the Viking Age.

Moreover, the Viking era is experiencing a renaissance in popular culture, with an increasing number of books, films, TV shows, and online content dedicated to the Vikings and their exploits. This resurgence of interest further emphasizes the lasting impact of the Vikings on the global imagination.

## The Sami People: Exploring Indigenous Culture and Traditions

As tourists venture into the captivating landscapes of Norway, they have the unique opportunity to explore the rich cultural heritage of the Sami people, the northernmost Indigenous community in Europe. The Sami have inhabited the region for thousands of years, and their traditions, customs, and way of life are deeply intertwined with the spectacular natural backdrop of the Far North. This comprehensive discussion will delve into the essential aspects of the Sami culture that tourists need to know to fully appreciate and respect the indigenous heritage they encounter during their travels.

### *The Joik Tradition: A Timeless Vocal Art*

The joik, a long-standing vocal tradition that maintains a special place in the hearts of the Sami, is at the center of their culture. Joik, also known as Sami folk music, is a distinctive style of singing that honors a person, an animal, or a location. The joik has miraculously endured the ages despite the Norwegian government's demands for acculturation and assimilation. In the 1950s, its use was outlawed in Sami area schools when it was declared to be sinful. The joik, however, has recently seen a resurgence as a result of numerous new musicians fusing it with diverse musical genres, including jazz, metal, and rock.

The Norwegian-Sami group KEiiNO, who represented Norway in the Eurovision Song Contest, has served as a testament to the joik's resurgence on the international arena. They successfully merged pop, electronica, dance, and joik in their song "Spirit in the Sky," which received a great deal of support and admiration from the general audience. The joik's status in contemporary culture is further cemented by the interpretations of other notable Norwegian artists, including Mari Boine and Frode Fjellheim.

### Sami Cultural Influences in Disney's Frozen

Beyond music, the Sami culture has resonances in unexpected places. Nordic music served as the basis for the Disney movie "Frozen," and the production team discovered Sami musician and composer Frode Fjellheim while conducting research in Norway. They worked together to write the song "Vuelie," which is a slightly modified version of the original song "Eatnemen Vuelie" by Fjellheim. This song skillfully incorporates the joik, which Fjellheim learned as a child, into the melodic fabric of the movie. For introducing the joik to Hollywood and displaying the diversity of Sami culture to a worldwide audience, Fjellheim's work has been lauded.

### Reindeer Husbandry: The Heart of Sami Culture

The care of reindeer has long been a significant aspect of Sami culture. These magnificent creatures are fundamental to their way of life, giving them food, clothes, and a variety of other necessities. Northern Norway, Trndelag, Mre og Romsdal in Fjord Norway, and Hedmark in Eastern

71

Norway are the main regions where Norwegian reindeer herding is carried out.

Approximately 3,000 individuals are currently employed in Sami reindeer husbandry, with 2,200 of them in Finnmark alone. They make a living by selling items made from reindeer. Reindeer skins are used to make mittens, shoes, and other leather goods, while reindeer meat, a regional speciality, is sold throughout Norway and overseas. A journey to Finnmark would not be complete without trying "bidos," a classic Sami meal prepared with slow-cooked reindeer meat, potatoes, and carrots.

### *Duodji: Celebrating Sami Handicrafts*

Sami culture is well known for its distinctive manifestations, and one of its most valued customs is duodji, or Sami handicraft. Tool, clothing, jewelry, and accessory handicrafts are all included in the category of duodji. The gorgeous natural surrounds are frequently reflected in these handcrafted products, which also hold profound cultural value. Tourists that participate in duodji have a rare chance to see the skill and creativity that have been passed down through the years within the Sami culture.

## Arts and Literature: A Creative Journey through Norwegian Expression

For tourists visiting Norway, immersing themselves in the realm of arts and literature offers a captivating and enriching experience. Norwegian expression through various art forms has deep roots, tracing back to prehistoric times and evolving with influences from the Vikings, Sami culture, and contemporary creativity. This comprehensive discussion will explore the fascinating journey through Norwegian art and literature, showcasing the country's rich cultural heritage, renowned artists, and literary achievements. As tourists embark on this creative voyage, they will encounter captivating petroglyphs, awe-inspiring Viking art, contemporary street art, world-class museums, and a literary tradition that sets Norway apart as a reading nation.

## Norwegian Art: A Tapestry of History

### Prehistoric Norwegian Art

The oldest threads in the tapestry-like history of Norwegian art date back to the prehistoric age. Petroglyphs (rock carvings) and pictographs are the two main types of prehistoric art found in Norway (rock paintings). These fascinating old paintings show scenes from ordinary life and historical events like hunting and fishing. The biggest collection of prehistoric art in both Norway and Northern Europe is found at the Alta Rock Art, which is situated in the municipality of Alta in northern Norway. Petroglyphs and pictographs found at the five main sites of Hjemmeluft, Kfjord, Amtmannsnes, Storsternen, and Transfarelv provide information about the native flora and practices of the time period. The Alta Museum, which offers an immersive exploration into the rich heritage of prehistoric Norwegian art, includes the Hjemmeluft petroglyphs.

*Viking Art: The Marriage of Function and Decoration*

The Vikings, known for their seafaring prowess and fierce reputation, were also accomplished artists. Viking art was unique in that it often adorned functional objects, such as doors, ship posts, and earspoons, marrying both utility and aesthetic. Intricate carvings and embellishments adorned these objects, showcasing the Vikings' craftsmanship and artistic flair. While many Viking artifacts are displayed in museums, several Viking art styles have been categorized, each named after the geographical location where objects of that style were found. Notable among these styles is the Oseberg style, named after artifacts found in Oseberg, dating back to the 9th century. Viking art has left an enduring legacy, and exploring Norway's Viking museums and living villages provides a deeper understanding of this fascinating period in history.

*Contemporary Norwegian Art Scene*

Today, Norway's art scene is vibrant and diverse, reflecting the country's contemporary creativity. Norwegian street art has gained prominence, transforming urban landscapes into colorful and thought-provoking canvases. Murals and graffiti grace walls, showcasing the talents of local and international artists. The street art movement has found acceptance, with numerous cities embracing it as an integral part of their cultural expression.

74

Beyond street art, Norwegian artists have achieved international acclaim, with names like Edvard Munch, renowned for his iconic painting "The Scream," being just one of many notable examples. The works of other contemporary artists have also captured global attention, contributing to the country's cultural identity and artistic legacy.

**Norwegian Literature: A Nation of Readers**

Norway has earned a reputation as a nation of avid readers, with Norwegians reading more than any other European nationality. This literary passion is evident in their award-winning libraries, charming book towns, and the widespread popularity of literature.

*Literary Traditions and World-Class Writers*

Norwegian literature boasts a rich tradition, with writers celebrated for their storytelling prowess and literary contributions. Henrik Ibsen, often regarded as one of the world's greatest playwrights, left an indelible mark on the literary world with plays like "A Doll's House" and "Peer Gynt." His influence on modern drama and storytelling remains profound.

Contemporary Norwegian authors continue to make waves globally. Notable names such as Karl Ove Knausgård, Jo Nesbø, and Hanne Ørstavik have captivated readers worldwide with their compelling narratives and unique storytelling styles.

*Literary Tourism: Exploring the Authors' World*

For true literature enthusiasts, Norway offers a treasure trove of literary tourism opportunities. Visitors can explore authors' homes, writers' centers, book towns, and literature houses scattered throughout the country. These places offer insight into the lives of literary icons and provide a deeper understanding of their works and creative processes.

*Thirst for Murders at Easter: A Quirky Literary Tradition*

Norwegians have a unique literary tradition of reading crime fiction, particularly murder mysteries, during the Easter holiday season. This peculiar habit has become a cultural phenomenon, where crime novels top bestseller lists during Easter. This literary quirk has become a cherished tradition, bringing communities together as they indulge in thrilling reads during the holiday season.

# Music and Festivals: Celebrating Norwegian Melodies and Cultural Events

Norway, a land of natural beauty and rich cultural heritage, also boasts a vibrant music scene and a plethora of festivals that celebrate Norwegian melodies and cultural events. From jazz festivals to medieval extravaganzas, Norway offers a diverse array of musical experiences that cater to all tastes. This comprehensive discussion will guide tourists through the musical landscape of Norway, exploring the country's major festivals, iconic events, and the unique charm of celebrating Norwegian culture through music.

## The Melodic Tapestry of Norwegian Festivals

Norway hosts a myriad of culture events throughout the year, enticing both locals and tourists with an exciting lineup of festivals, concerts, and exhibitions. These events showcase the best of Norwegian music and arts and provide visitors with an unforgettable experience that transcends beyond the capital, Oslo, to embrace the entire country.

*Constitution Day: A Celebration of Norwegian Identity*

Constitution Day, observed on May 17, is one of Norway's most important national holidays. This celebration marks the signing of the country's constitution in 1814, solidifying its independence and identity. On this day, the streets come alive with parades, performances, and festivities. Visitors can witness the fervor of national pride as Norwegians don traditional costumes called "bunads" and march through the streets with joyous exuberance. Constitution Day is an excellent opportunity for tourists to immerse themselves in the heart of Norwegian culture and witness the unison of tradition and modernity.

*Grieg in Bergen: A Tribute to a Musical Maestro*

The Grieg in Bergen festival, held from July 31 to August 17, pays homage to Norway's greatest composer, Edvard Grieg. The festival features a series of concerts that showcase Grieg's timeless compositions, including his famous "Peer Gynt" suite and piano concerto. Set against the stunning backdrop of Bergen, this festival provides an enchanting experience, blending music and nature in perfect harmony. Tourists can delve into the genius of Grieg and witness the profound impact of his music on the Norwegian cultural landscape.

*Oslo Jazz Festival: A Rhapsody of Rhythms*

For jazz aficionados, the Oslo Jazz Festival, taking place from August 13 to 19, is a must-attend event. This annual celebration brings together a diverse lineup of jazz artists from Norway and beyond, creating an eclectic medley of styles and sounds. From intimate club performances to open-air concerts in scenic locations, the festival promises an unforgettable experience for all music enthusiasts. Tourists can embrace the magic of jazz as they soak in the lively atmosphere and groove to the rhythms of this beloved genre.

**A Tapestry of Music Festivals Across Norway**

*Bergen International Festival: An Extravaganza of Arts*

The Bergen International Festival, held from May 24 to June 7, is a grand celebration of arts and culture. This prestigious festival showcases an array of concerts, ballets, operas, and theater performances, captivating audiences with a diverse lineup of artistic expressions. Set in the picturesque city of Bergen, the festival's enchanting venues complement the world-class performances, creating an immersive experience for festival-goers. Visitors can witness the convergence of talent and creativity on display during this cultural extravaganza.

*Gladmat Festival: A Feast for the Senses*

The Gladmat Festival, held from June 28 to July 1 in Stavanger, is a culinary delight that tantalizes taste buds with an array of delicious flavors. This food festival showcases the best of Norwegian cuisine, featuring traditional dishes and innovative creations prepared by talented chefs. With an emphasis on local and sustainable ingredients, the Gladmat Festival highlights Norway's culinary heritage and its commitment to gastronomic excellence. Tourists can indulge in a gastronomic journey, savoring the tastes and aromas that define Norwegian food culture.

*Bergenfest: Rock, Pop, Hip Hop, and Folk Music*

Bergenfest, held from June 14 to 17, is a music festival that caters to diverse musical tastes. From rock and pop to hip hop and folk, this festival brings together a lineup of international and Norwegian artists, creating an electrifying atmosphere of music and camaraderie. Set against the scenic backdrop of Bergen, the festival offers a unique experience, where tourists can immerse themselves in a medley of genres and performances, all within the vibrant atmosphere of Norway's second-largest city.

Music and festivals in Norway provide tourists with a captivating glimpse into the country's cultural tapestry and the vibrancy of its creative spirit. From jazz festivals and rock extravaganzas to culinary feasts and celebrations of national pride, Norway's music and cultural events offer a unique blend of tradition, innovation, and artistic excellence. For travelers seeking an immersive experience into Norwegian melodies and cultural celebrations, these festivals are a gateway to the heart and soul of the country's artistic heritage.

Other notable festivals include.

- Øya Festival, Oslo: A popular music festival featuring top musicians and bands in genres like indie, hip-hop, and electronic music. Visitors can enjoy live music performances and immerse themselves in the energetic atmosphere.
- Nordlysfestivalen, Tromsø: The Northern Lights Music Festival, featuring a celebration of music with concerts and master classes. Music lovers can enjoy a variety of musical genres and witness performances by talented musicians.
- The Peer Gynt Festival: Based on Henrik Ibsen's dramatic poem, the festival brings to life the story of Peer Gynt through theater productions. Visitors can experience the finest theater performances and immerse themselves in the recreation of traditions.
- Saint Lucia's Day: Celebrated on December 13, this festival marks the arrival of Christmas and features singing of songs and traditional processions with girls dressed as Saint Lucia carrying lights.
- The Polar Jazz Festival: Held in the northernmost part of Norway,

this festival attracts jazz lovers and music enthusiasts alike. Visitors can enjoy jazz performances by both professionals and local musicians, showcasing their skills.

- Midnight Sun Marathon, Tromsø: a special marathon that takes place in the summer when the sun never sets. The gorgeous route and the unique experience of jogging in the midnight sun are available to participants.

- Trondheim Jazz Festival: One of the oldest jazz festivals in Europe, featuring a lineup of national and international jazz artists. Visitors can enjoy jazz concerts, jam sessions, and workshops held at various venues in Trondheim.

- Arctic Sounds Festival, Harstad: A winter music festival held in a unique Arctic setting, showcasing a mix of genres like pop, rock, and electronic music. Visitors can experience live performances, outdoor activities, and the magical winter ambiance.

- Oslo World Music Festival: A multicultural festival celebrating music and diversity, featuring artists from around the world. Visitors can enjoy concerts, workshops, and cultural events representing various music traditions.

- Tromsø International Film Festival (TIFF): An influential film festival focusing on new and emerging filmmakers, as well as Arctic and Northern-themed films. Visitors can attend film screenings, discussions, and industry events.

- Norsk Rakfiskfestival, Valdres: A unique festival celebrating rakfisk, a traditional Norwegian dish of fermented fish. Visitors can taste different varieties of rakfisk, participate in cooking competitions, and enjoy cultural performances and exhibitions.

## Culinary Delights: Tasting Traditional Norwegian Cuisine

Norway's culinary landscape is a delightful tapestry of traditional dishes deeply rooted in its environment and history. The country's long coastline provides an abundance of fresh fish, while its cold mountain air preserves meats like reindeer and lamb. From hearty stews to unique cheeses, Norwegian cuisine offers a gastronomic journey for food enthusiasts. In this comprehensive guide, we will explore ten must-try local cuisines that showcase the best of Norway's traditional fare and ten top restaurants where travelers can savor these culinary delights.

### Ten Must-Try Local Cuisines

- Frikl: The western regions of Norway love this hearty stew in the winter. It is simple to prepare and ideal for the colder months because it is made with lamb, cabbage, and black pepper.
- Pickled herring, known as sursild, is a delicacy that can be purchased in practically every supermarket and is a staple of Scandinavian cuisine. Additionally, there are other methods to consume this delectable fish, such as fried herring.
- Finnbiff: This dish, made with sautéed reindeer meat and served in a flavorful sauce, is common in the northern regions of Norway.
- Kjttkaker: Kjttkaker is a straightforward yet tasty Norwegian dish served with brown sauce, potatoes, and carrots. It is similar to meatballs.

- Smalahove (Sheep's Head) is a traditional dish made of a sheep's head that has been boiled or steam-cooked for many hours and served with rutabaga and potatoes. It is not typically eaten on weekdays.

- Brunost (Brown Cheese): The most popular varieties of brown cheese in Norway, such as Gudbrandsdalsost or Mysost, are frequently eaten on sandwiches or crispbread. The brown color of these cheeses is caused by heated milk sugars used in their manufacturing.

- Salmon that has been cured in salt, sugar, and dill to create gravlaks, a classic salmon preparation, produces a savory dish that is frequently served with potatoes, vegetables, and sauce.

- Lutefisk is a whitefish dish that is typically consumed around Christmastime. It is created using lye and cod that has been dried and salted.

- Sodd: A traditional mutton soup with potatoes and carrots that captures the flavor of real Norwegian soups.

- Danish Waffles: These heart-shaped waffles are a popular snack in Norway and a pleasant way to end a dinner. They are frequently eaten with brunost.

**Ten Top Restaurants**

- **Maaemo, Oslo**: A three-star Michelin restaurant, Maaemo offers an exceptional dining experience with expertly crafted and memorable dishes in a dramatic, high-ceilinged dining room.

- **RE-NAA, Stavanger**: Another Michelin-starred restaurant, RE-NAA offers a two-star dining experience worth a detour, showcasing exceptional culinary artistry.
- **À L'aise, Oslo**: This restaurant received one Michelin star and the Welcome and Service Award, presenting traditional Norwegian dishes with a modern touch.
- **Sabi Omakase, Stavanger**: A one-star Michelin restaurant, Sabi Omakase offers a unique and immersive dining experience centered around omakase-style dining.
- **Under, Lindesnes**: This one-star Michelin restaurant stands out for its extraordinary underwater dining experience, where guests can savor seafood delicacies in a stunning underwater setting.
- **Bare, Bergen**: Offering a Michelin-starred experience, Bare specializes in modern Nordic cuisine that celebrates local ingredients and flavors.
- **Lysverket, Bergen**: Another Michelin-starred restaurant in Bergen, Lysverket presents a creative menu inspired by Norwegian culinary traditions.
- **Speilsalen, Trondheim**: This one-star Michelin restaurant in Trondheim offers a refined dining experience with an emphasis on culinary artistry.
- **Fagn, Trondheim**: Also boasting a Michelin star, Fagn combines Nordic and Japanese influences to create innovative and delightful dishes.
- **Statholdergaarden, Oslo**: This Michelin-starred restaurant in Oslo serves exquisite dishes in an elegant and historic setting.

3. **If you haven't already done so, scan the QR code at the beginning of the book** and download THE SPECIALIZED TRIPS AND UNIQUE EXPERIENCES IN NORWAY IN OUR EBOOK
4. **Scan the QR code below and <u>leave quick feedback on Amazon!</u>**

# SCAN ME

# Chapter 5:

# Accommodation Options in Norway

Norway, with its breathtaking natural beauty and diverse landscapes, is a dream destination for travelers seeking unique and immersive experiences. From the vibrant city of Oslo to serene fjord-side retreats and charming coastal villages, Norway offers a wide range of accommodation options to suit every traveler's preferences and budget. Whether you seek urban comforts, tranquility in nature, or an adventurous glamping experience, Norway has it all. In this comprehensive guide, we will explore various accommodation options under the following subheadings:

**Oslo and Urban Comforts**

As the capital and largest city of Norway, Oslo offers a plethora of accommodation options to cater to diverse traveler needs. From luxury hotels to budget-friendly hostels, visitors can find suitable places to stay in this vibrant city. Travelers looking for urban comforts and convenience will find plenty of options in the city center. Popular areas to stay include:

- **Karl Johans gate**: This iconic street in Oslo is home to many hotels, restaurants, and shops. Staying here gives you easy access to major attractions like the Royal Palace and Oslo Cathedral.
- **Aker Brygge**: This waterfront area is known for its trendy restaurants, bars, and shops. Hotels in this area offer stunning views of the harbor and the Oslo Fjord.
- **Grünerløkka**: This trendy neighborhood is famous for its vibrant arts and culture scene. It offers a variety of boutique hotels and guesthouses, perfect for those seeking a more local experience.
- **Sentrum**: The central district of Oslo offers a mix of accommodation options, from luxury hotels to budget-friendly hostels. It is an excellent base for exploring the city's main attractions.

### Fjord-side Retreats: Immersion in Tranquility

Norway's fjords are some of the country's most picturesque natural wonders, and staying in a fjord-side retreat allows visitors to immerse themselves in the tranquility of these breathtaking landscapes. Many fjord-side accommodations offer stunning views of the water and surrounding mountains. Popular fjords for accommodation include:

87

- **Sognefjord**: Norway's longest and deepest fjord, Sognefjord, is surrounded by majestic mountains and charming villages. Accommodations here range from cozy guesthouses to luxurious hotels.

- **Geirangerfjord**: Known for its dramatic cliffs and waterfalls, Geirangerfjord is a UNESCO World Heritage Site. Visitors can find comfortable lodges and cabins along its shores.

- **Nærøyfjord**: Another UNESCO-listed fjord, Nærøyfjord, offers a serene escape with accommodation options that blend seamlessly with the surrounding nature.

## Quaint Coastal Villages and Seaside Escapes

Norway's coastline is dotted with charming coastal villages that offer a glimpse into traditional Norwegian life. Staying in these villages allows travelers to experience the country's maritime culture and enjoy stunning sea views. Some picturesque coastal villages with accommodation options include:

- **Ålesund**: Famous for its Art Nouveau architecture, Ålesund is a picturesque coastal town with several charming hotels and guesthouses.

- **Bergen**: Norway's second-largest city, Bergen, boasts a historic harbor district called Bryggen. Visitors can find hotels with views of the colorful wooden houses and the sea.

- **Lofoten Islands**: A collection of rugged islands in northern Norway, Lofoten offers a range of accommodation options, from traditional fisherman's cabins to boutique hotels.

## Mountain Cabins and Wilderness Lodges

For those seeking a rustic and immersive experience in Norway's wilderness, staying in mountain cabins or wilderness lodges is an excellent choice. These accommodations offer access to some of the country's most remote and stunning landscapes. Some options include:

- **Jotunheimen National Park**: Known as the "Home of the Giants," Jotunheimen offers a range of mountain cabins and lodges for hikers and nature enthusiasts.
- **Rondane National Park**: Norway's oldest national park, Rondane, is a popular destination for hiking and cross-country skiing. Accommodations include wilderness lodges and mountain cabins.
- **Hardangervidda National Park**: Europe's largest mountain plateau, Hardangervidda, offers wilderness lodges and cabins for those seeking a true wilderness experience.

## Hotels near Major Attractions

Many of Norway's major attractions are located in or near popular tourist destinations. Visitors can find hotels and lodges that offer easy access to these iconic sights. Some examples include:

- **The Northern Lights**: Tromsø and the Lofoten Islands are popular spots for witnessing the mesmerizing Northern Lights, and accommodations here offer optimal viewing opportunities.

- **The Midnight Sun**: The North Cape and Svalbard are ideal locations for experiencing the Midnight Sun phenomenon during the summer months.
- **Bryggen**: Staying near Bryggen in Bergen allows visitors to explore this historic harbor district and its UNESCO-listed wooden buildings.

## Camping and Glamping Experiences

For adventurous travelers who want to get closer to nature, Norway offers numerous camping and glamping experiences. From camping in the wilderness to luxury glamping tents, these accommodations provide unique and unforgettable experiences. Some options include:

- **National Parks**: Many national parks in Norway offer designated camping areas where visitors can pitch tents and enjoy the tranquility of nature.
- **Glamping Sites**: Several glamping sites across Norway offer luxurious tents with comfortable amenities, allowing travelers to enjoy the great outdoors without sacrificing comfort.

## Vacation Rentals and Holiday Homes

Vacation rentals and holiday homes are an excellent option for families and groups traveling together. They offer the convenience of a home away from home and are available in various locations across Norway. Popular platforms like Airbnb and Vrbo offer a wide selection of vacation rentals.

## Budget-friendly Hostels for Backpackers

For budget-conscious travelers, hostels provide affordable and social accommodation options. Norway has a good network of hostels, particularly in major cities and popular tourist destinations. Backpackers can find shared dormitories or private rooms at reasonable rates.

Norway's diverse landscapes and natural wonders offer a wide range of accommodation options for tourists. From urban comforts in Oslo to fjord-side retreats, quaint coastal villages, mountain cabins, and wilderness lodges, there is something to suit every traveler's taste and budget. Whether you prefer immersing yourself in tranquil fjords, witnessing the Northern Lights, or experiencing glamping in the wilderness, Norway's accommodation options promise an unforgettable and authentic travel experience.

# Chapter 6:
# Practical Tips and Useful
# Information

Norway, with its awe-inspiring landscapes, majestic fjords, and vibrant cities, attracts tourists from around the world seeking unforgettable experiences. To make the most of your journey in Norway, it's essential to be well-prepared and informed about transportation options, budget and expenses, safety and health guidelines, and sustainable travel practices. We will provide practical tips for tourists in Norway under the following subheadings:

## Transportation in Norway: Car Rentals, Public Transport, and Getting Around

Norway offers a well-developed transportation network that includes various modes of transport, ensuring seamless connections across the country. Whether you prefer exploring the scenic fjords by boat, traversing the rugged landscapes by train, or venturing into remote areas by car, Norway's transportation options cater to different travel preferences. Here are some key transportation tips:

- **Public Transport**: Norway's public transport system is extensive and efficient, comprising buses, trains, and ferries. EnTur is a helpful national public transport planner that provides route information, although tickets are often purchased directly from service operators. Buses are a budget-friendly option for traveling in rural areas, while trains offer reliability and scenic journeys. Advance booking for train tickets can result in significant savings, so plan ahead to get the best deals.

- **Ferries**: Traveling by boat is one of the most scenic ways to experience Norway's stunning fjords. Ferries transport cars, foot passengers, and cyclists, offering breathtaking views of the surrounding landscapes. The famous Hurtigruten coastal ferry provides premium cruise packages but also allows booking individual legs of the journey.

- **Car Rentals**: Renting a car provides flexibility and access to remote areas. However, driving in Norway can be expensive due to vehicle hire, toll roads, ferry crossings, and fuel costs. Consider renting locally for a few days instead of the entire trip to save money. Ensure you have an international driving license and check the availability of automatic or manual transmission cars.

- **Cycling**: For the adventurous and eco-conscious travelers, cycling offers an immersive experience. Norway has cycling routes and contacts for enthusiasts seeking to explore the country on two wheels.

## Budget and Expenses: Money-Saving Tips and Deals

Norway is renowned for its natural beauty, but it's also known for its relatively high cost of living. To make the most of your trip without breaking the bank, consider the following money-saving tips:

- **Discount Fares**: Look for discounted advance fares, often known as "minipris tickets," which can significantly reduce the cost of long-distance journeys on trains. Booking tickets well in advance can result in substantial savings.
- **Travel Passes**: Consider investing in the Norway Eurail Pass, which allows unlimited rail travel within a specific duration. Additionally, explore the "Explore Norway Ticket" offered by Wideroe, which provides regional flight passes.
- **Group and Family Discounts**: If traveling in a group or with family, inquire about concessionary fares and reductions for children, senior citizens, and disabled travelers.

- **Off-Peak Travel**: Avoid peak tourist seasons and explore Norway during the shoulder seasons to find better deals on accommodations and activities.

## Safety and Health: Guidelines for a Secure and Healthy Journey

Norway is generally considered a safe destination for travelers, but it's essential to prioritize safety and health during your journey:

- **Emergency Numbers**: Familiarize yourself with emergency numbers, including police, medical assistance, and fire services.
- **Travel Insurance**: Get thorough travel insurance that includes coverage for lost or stolen items, trip cancellations, and medical emergencies.
- **Weather Precautions**: The weather in Norway can be erratic, especially in the countryside. Before going outside, be sure to bring the right clothing and equipment and to keep up with the weather.
- **Health Precautions**: Ensure you have all necessary vaccinations and medications, and carry a basic first-aid kit.
- **Natural Hazards**: Be aware of potential natural hazards, such as slippery trails, wildlife encounters, and sudden weather changes.

## Sustainable Travel in Norway: Eco-Friendly Choices and

## Responsible Tourism

Norway is committed to sustainable tourism practices and responsible travel. As a visitor, you can contribute to preserving the country's pristine nature and cultural heritage:

- **Public Transport**: Opt for eco-friendly public transport options, such as trains and buses, to minimize your carbon footprint.
- **Eco-Friendly Accommodations**: Choose environmentally conscious accommodations that prioritize sustainability and responsible practices.
- **Leave No Trace**: Respect nature and wildlife by adhering to the principles of "Leave No Trace." Avoid littering, stay on marked trails, and observe wildlife from a distance.
- **Support Local Businesses**: Contribute to the local economy by supporting small businesses, artisans, and locally-owned shops.
- **Respect Local Culture**: Familiarize yourself with local customs and traditions, and always be respectful to the local population and their way of life.

Traveling in Norway offers an unforgettable experience, and by following these practical tips, you can make the most of your journey while staying within your budget and ensuring a safe and sustainable trip. Whether you're exploring the country's natural wonders, immersing yourself in the vibrant urban centers, or venturing into remote

# Conclusion

As our captivating journey through Norway comes to a close, we are left spellbound by the country's breathtaking landscapes, rich cultural heritage, and warm hospitality. Norway, a land of dramatic fjords, picturesque villages, and vibrant cities, offers an unparalleled travel experience that captivates the hearts of all who venture into its embrace.

One of the must-see wonders of Norway is undoubtedly the majestic fjords. The Geirangerfjord and Nærøyfjord, with their towering cliffs and crystal-clear waters, leave visitors in awe of nature's grandeur. Exploring these fjords is an unforgettable experience, whether you choose to embark on a serene fjord cruise, paddle through the waters on a kayaking tour, or take a scenic hike to immerse yourself fully in the unique landscapes.

Norway's cities also hold their own charm, each offering distinct experiences. Oslo, a city of cultural treasures and natural beauty, invites you to explore its historic landmarks, world-class museums, and lush green spaces. The Akerhus fortress, Viking Ship Museum, and Vigeland Sculpture Park are just a few highlights that beckon travelers to uncover the city's rich heritage.

Bergen, nestled amidst scenic fjords, captivates with its charming fish market, historic Gamle Bergen, and Mount Fløyen's panoramic views. Meanwhile, Trondheim's colorful buildings and laid-back atmosphere create a perfect destination for those seeking a delightful mix of culture and nightlife.

Venturing further north, Lofoten awaits, offering a picturesque paradise of mountains, wildlife, and a slower pace of life. The Northern Lights shimmering in the night sky reflect in the tranquil waters, creating a magical display that photographers and dreamers alike cherish.

Norway's commitment to sustainability and eco-friendly practices makes it a frontrunner in responsible tourism. The capital city, Oslo, stands as an example of progress, as it aims to be a net-zero emissions city by 2030, with a fully-electric public transit system already in operation. Visitors can immerse themselves in Norway's pristine landscapes while knowing their travel choices contribute to preserving its natural beauty for future generations.

Looking forward, 2023 offers exciting additions to Norway's attractions. The National Museum in Oslo presents captivating exhibitions that celebrate art, design, and architecture, while the allure of Troll tourism, inspired by the hit Netflix movie, promises to unveil the country's untamed nature in a new light.

For those with a sense of adventure, Svalbard's remote beauty awaits on the new small ship expedition cruise, MV Vikingfjord. Witnessing the spectacular Northern Lights is another must-do, with experts predicting a season of intensified aurora displays, creating unforgettable memories under the dancing night sky.

As this Norway travel guide comes to an end, we bid you farewell, armed with insider tips and a sense of wanderlust to embark on your Norwegian adventure. Whether you seek the tranquility of the fjords, the charm of cities, or the thrill of witnessing nature's marvels, Norway promises to fulfill your every desire. Embrace the warmth of its people, the vastness of its landscapes, and the magic that lies within every corner. In Norway, every moment is an invitation to explore, discover, and be captivated by the sheer beauty of the Scandinavian paradise. Welcome to Norway – where dreams meet reality in an enchanting harmony of nature and culture.

1. **If you haven't already done so, scan the QR code at the beginning of the book** and download THE SPECIALIZED TRIPS AND UNIQUE EXPERIENCES IN NORWAY IN OUR EBOOK
2. **Scan the QR code below and <u>leave quick feedback on Amazon!</u>**

# SCAN ME

Made in United States
Orlando, FL
15 September 2024

51537332R00057